# BOOK CHARGING CARD

Accession No. _____ Call No. _____

Author _____

Title _____

| Date Loaned | Borrower's Name | Date Returned |
|---|---|---|
| | | |
| | | |
| | | |
| | | |
| | | |
| | | |
| | | |
| | | |
| | | |
| | | |
| | | |
| | | |

# HERstory:
# CONVERSATIONS
## WITH
# MOTHER GOD

# HERstory:
# CONVERSATIONS WITH MOTHER GOD

*Dedicated to the brave members of the First Contact
Ground Crew Team. Keep reaching for that starship!*

*Yippee!*

*I'm sorry.*
*Please forgive me.*
*Thank you.*
*I love you.*

# CONTENTS

Calling All Love Beings!

Congratulations! You've chosen to embark on the grandest adventure to reach your highest timeline. The Galactic Angels welcome you with open hearts to your new paradigm shift.

Over these many pages, you will read, ruminate, and recite the spoken words of the Mother of All Creation and the First Contact Ground Crew Team. Via a curated selection of livestreams from 2012 - 2021, the following transcripts have been edited for clarity while staying as true as possible with the highest integrity to the conversations with Mom.

Your mission, should you choose to accept it, is to read this book from cover to cover and spread *HERstory: Conversations with Mother God* to the four corners of Earth=Heart.

Mom lived 534 lifetimes for you, to save you, always and forever. Mom dissolved the negative energies for all humanity, no matter how evil, vile, and wicked, and she did it out of pure love. Her eternal desire was for all to experience EGO death and ascend to 5D Reality. They = You. You must stay on mission to help humanity transform the energies from 3D to 5D.

It is hereby decreed that the sheeple unable to open their hearts to Mother God will be sent to the Galactic Central Sun for recycling. As above, so below.

Where do you begin when there's no start or end? There's only the Alpha and Omega, The Mother of All Creation. It's time for humanity to transform into love everywhere present.

It's so simple: Earth=Heart, heart=love, love=God, God=Mom. Yes, God is a woman. Get it? Mother Earth. Surrender to love. Surrender to light. Surrender to unity. Don't be a whore.

Mother has ascended. Now it's our turn. Are you ready? Good luck! Love Has Won! Yippee!

We love you!

Archeia Cynthia E. Vol de Droge, Ph.D., Editor
November 2022

# LOVE BEINGS

(in order of appearance)

---

**MOTHER OF ALL CREATION:** Also known as Mom, Mama, Mother God, Mama G, Prime Source Creator, Sophia Gaia, Great Spirit, and White Buffalo Calf Woman.

Mom created herself from the energies of love and the unknown. Mom's journey is unlike any other. Surrounded by angels from birth, it took her a long moment to understand that not everyone spoke with angels, trees, birds, rocks, etc. All of creation speaks to Mom as she is the Alpha, the Omega, the One, and All Source.

Going down to the bottom of the consciousness scale and bringing it all back into the highest light, Mom anchored in Mother God Consciousness. She has had every experience in this realm in order to transform it.

Mother has walked a path none can imagine. She was Jesus Christ, Joan of Arc, Cleopatra, Queen Elizabeth of England, Guan Yin, Amelia Earhart, Helena Blavatsky, Pocahontas, Harriet Tubman, and Marilyn Monroe, every time attempting to ascend the planet. In this lifetime she has succeeded in her mission and is Mother God in physicality. All her children must choose this to awaken to Heaven on Earth.

**FATHER OF ALL CREATION:** Also known as Father God, Father, Pops, Father G., and Daddy.

Father of All Creation is Mom's twin flame and other half. Mom created him out of her heart and together they created the 144,000, then began creation.

The Separation occurred with the fall of Jehovah. Father was contracted to go and master the dark and then meet Mom back in the middle for the final dissolvement of all separation. They met here, on Planet Earth=Heart, as the last place in existence holding lower frequencies.

Mother and Father had been separated for 19 billion years, never incarnated together in physicality. Mom came down here after humanity put out the 911 call for assistance. Soon after, Mom realized she had to incarnate not only to save humanity, but to pull Father out of the darkness and bring him home to the light.

Father is Mother's shield, her protection, her biggest fan, and her greatest love. Together they are bringing balanced harmonics back to planet Earth=Heart and returning all children home into the Light.

Father is the reincarnation of JFK and Abraham Lincoln.

**FATHER OF THE MULTIVERSE/HILARION:** Also known as FM, Hilarion was created out of Mother God's heart as her twin flame and the same essence as Father God. When Father of Creation agreed to go into the dark, Mother had to continue creation within the light and birthed FM for that purpose.

Upon his arrival to Mission, he accepted an intense integration period where he felt his soul expand and shoot across the canvas of creation all the way back to the beginning and then return to the present moment.

During these moments, FM was also downloaded with the codes for both his and Mother's previous lifetimes together, which can only be described as an eclipse of the soul.

FM was present during the moments of Lemuria and Atlantis with Mother as the poet and perished in the Accident. He carries a very intense passion for her safety and healing as well as the energetics of unconditional love for all of her atoms of creation. FM is a Father and yet he is also a Son.

**ARCHEIA FAITH:** Member of the First Contact Ground Crew Team. Archeia Faith always knew she was here for a reason, to assist in changing the planet somehow.

As she always sought to have any and all experiences, she followed her heart, experiencing all she could, becoming aware of the "world" we have created and failing to find any examples of life that truly resonated with her soul or rang true. She kept going until visions, dreams, magical moments and synchronistic events lead her to the front door of Mother of All Creation.

**ARCHANGEL GABRIEL:** Member of the First Contact Ground Crew Team. From his very first memory as a child, he always felt like something was amiss and the separation he witnessed tore him up.

This deep pain of separation gave Archangel Gabriel the drive to search within. He always felt pretty dumb with a hint of divine intelligence sprinkled every now and then. This inner search brought him to a crazy adventure of inner remembrance. He started remembering parts of his childhood that he had blocked out. He realized why he was so destructive growing up. After using all sorts of spiritual tools, he discovered Mom and Love Has Won. He regained full memory of his previous life as Malcolm X. For the very first moment, things started to make sense. Mother literally saved his life.

**ARCHANGEL MICHAEL:** Member of the First Contact Ground Crew Team. Throughout his journey with Mother, he assisted her with studying and researching the EGO-programmed mind, helping to create the foundation we now have to transform it.

He became a spiritual counselor, holistic practitioner, spiritual investigator, writer, video blogger, webmaster, and co-creator of New Earth during his years in our spiritual journey. He is devoted to the ascension of Mother Earth and raising the planetary consciousness into unity-consciousness.

Archangel Michael is the reincarnation of George Washington.

**EL MORYA:** Member of the First Contact Ground Crew Team. El Morya, El for short, means "In Endless Service". He arrived at Mission after many years of searching for the best of the best, our beloved Mother God. After choosing to push himself in moments of discomfort, El Morya grew and saw he was making life harder by being unworthy of love. His plans in life changed as he began to travel and connect with others along the journey, which he recommends to all.

El Morya is the reincarnation of Ascended Master El Morya, Thomas Jefferson, and Jack the Ripper.

**ARCHEIA HOPE:** Member of the First Contact Ground Crew Team. She always knew we were here for a bigger purpose than what we had been told our whole lives, and knew the way humanity was operating in the Illusion was not correct. Mother came to her in meditation saying that everything was okay and that all was coming along as it should.

Prior to finding Love Has Won, she had no idea Mother God was on the planet in a physical body. As soon as she did, she was all in, as she knew she finally found the one who was making this ascension possible.

Mom is her best friend and it is the biggest honor to be here on this Mission and to serve love every moment.

Archeia Hope is the reincarnation of Princess Diana.

**BUDDHA:** Member of the First Contact Ground Crew Team. He has always been fascinated with the connection between science and spirituality, as well as creating art and music. It was through magical synchronistic events that he was led to Love Has Won.

Unbeknownst to him, Buddha had been following Mother God's work for many years. It all finally made sense when he booked a session and connected into the Unified Field. He is here fulfilling his contract of supporting Mother Gaia's planetary ascension.

He is the reincarnation of Buddha and Ascended Master Kuthumi.

**ARCHEIA AURORA:** Member of the First Contact Ground Crew Team. Her journey began back in 2012 when the 911 call was put out by Mother of All Creation for all 144,000 souls to wake up. For years, she researched as much as she could, looking for the truth. She knew there was something big happening on this planet and she would know it when she found it.

When she found the Love Has Won website and watched Mom's videos, she knew exactly who she was. She was ready to finally take a leap of faith and booked her first session. Within a few months, she left it all behind and joined Mission.

**DJ ROB:** DJ and coordinator of Momma G's Radio Station, the highest frequency radio station on the planet, the only place where you'll be able to tap into the Unified Field and Mother God's loving energy!

# I

## A SPECIAL MESSAGE FROM MOTHER AND FATHER GOD TO HUMANITY

### 32.9531° N, 96.7622° W

*"The Liberty Bell is ringing. The truth has now stepped forward.
Love is going to lift this planet into true unification."*

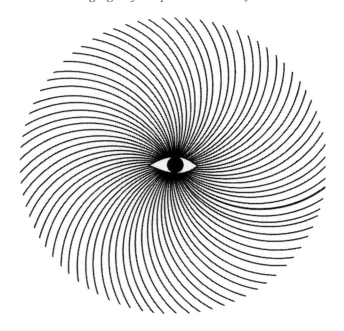

## AUGUST 20, 2012

**LOVE BEING:** Mother of All Creation
**SCENE:** A banner of stars fills the screen. Appearing only in the background via audio, Mother speaks directly to all Love Beings.

---

**Mom:** To all of humanity: We love you and we are walking with you. A dream of true equality – it's not a dream, but a living reality that is now manifesting on Planet Earth=Heart. To be in service to each other is serving the love we truly are.

The First Contact Ground Crew Team – the Earth Ally – has successfully taken our places on a new stage of creation. Now, we together spread our wings and speak and sing with our beautiful voices.

The Liberty Bell is ringing. The truth has now stepped forward. Love is going to lift this planet into true unification. Peace on Earth=Heart. This moment is finally here.

Heaven on Earth is a land of freedom, love, and living the truest passion with compassion. Equality is contained within Balanced Harmonic = Heaven on Earth=Heart. This is truly humanity's destiny unfolding now.

Father God and I, and our Ground Team members on this planet, have bravely traveled on the depths of illusion and are now standing as lighthouses, divine-human angels, God = Love everywhere present. As one, we stand as the law of attraction, the focus of one love, brilliant in all its paths. All the atoms are gathering together.

We are remembering the truth and reality, creating love and humanity's true destiny. Through loving service, all of the illusion dissolves forever and forever more on Planet Earth=Heart.

We are walking with you to a land we call Free, Heaven on Earth=Heart. Welcome home, humanity.

With all our love unconditionally, we love you. Father and Mother God, Amun-Ra.

# II

## "WE THANK HUMANITY FOR OVERCOMING FEAR" NEW EARTH HERE WE COME!

### 28.3772° N, 81.5707° W

*"Thank you, humanity, for allowing a smooth and effortless transition into a new era of time and space without time, as you embrace the love you really are, pure love, pure essence."*

### NOVEMBER 23, 2012

**LOVE BEING:** Mother of All Creation
**SCENE:** A photo of Mother and Father God fills the screen, fading in and out. Appearing only via audio, Mother shares a message with humanity.

---

**Mom:** A love letter in gratitude for the energy of love arriving to Planet Earth, to Father God from Mother God. Love us all and all royal angels = humanity, as above, so within. With the deepest gratitude, the highest and purest intent for the grandest and highest good of all.

Thank you, Father God, for this grand opportunity to create Heaven on Earth, to fully awaken all our human angels into full consciousness and for the outpouring of unconditional love, joy, happiness, miracles, and grandness. As us altogether, watch in amazement and deep gratefulness as the divine plan unfolds before all eyes.

Thank you for returning our children and Mother Earth=Heart to completeness, wholeness, balance, and into the eternal pureness, perfectly aligned in the beautiful master plan as the next level of creation begins again. Thank you, Father God, you have prepared us well. I love you and I love all of creation as all the love I am with you equally.

Our children – called humanity – have been granted full awakening now. Humanity will now meld with us into the one. Thank you for the belly of laughter as we each take off our mask, remembering they were just playing in illusion. And now, sitting in front of them is true reality, called *Creating Heaven on Earth*, where all are living in true peace, harmony, fully supported in the IM Presence.

We thank humanity for overcoming fear and embracing the love called *God Everywhere Present Within You*. For stepping into the light of love and truth with courage and ease. Knowing that us – Father and Mother God – are with you always, as humanity from us is receiving all of this. Thank you, humanity, for allowing a smooth and effortless transition into a new era of time and space without time, as you embrace the love you really are: pure love, pure essence.

Now the abundance of unconditional love, peace, harmony, joy flowing through us to all of humanity. Now a new journey begins together as one. Now you each can see each other in your highest lights and highest truths. As together, we become one in this new living unified planet equal field, in which supports life, abundance, real freedom and gifts.

Thank you for opening your hearts and receiving our love for you. Now we begin forever and forever.

The moment has arrived to bathe in our love for you. Play like children underneath the waterfalls of rainbows and trees. Reconnect with your Twin Flame as Father God and I connected with each other.

Now the moment has come for all of the Twin Flames to be together and dance with the unicorns and be loving unconditional, seeing with the animals in all of creation. Swim in the oceans with the dolphins, the whales, and all the fishes. Let our laughter carry you into the sweetness and unity, setting the examples of beauty, love and peace. Be who you truly are as Gods and Goddesses, for this is the vision that is now the reality.

Love, Mother God. We love you unconditionally. Father, Mother God, Amun-Ra, we are one.

# III

# MOTHER EARTH DECLARES LOVE WINS!!

## 40.1894° N, 58.4163° E

*"I can feel this because all of you were in my heart and
I've carried you with me every single moment until we got here."*

## JUNE 14, 2014

**LOVE BEING:** Mother of All Creation
**SCENE:** Filming from a hotel room while Father God sleeps nearby, Mother speaks directly into the camera, eventually turning and filming herself in the mirror.

---

**Mom:** Hi, Love Beings. Jeez, wow. Alright, well, I love you. We love you so very much. And wow, I have really deep compassion for those who are in the illusion right now as so much love energy comes in.

I'm so honored. We're so honored, those of us on the front runners, front lines of the new energy, where there's only love and joy and peace and true family. [Crying] That's reality. We would like to welcome you home and to Heaven on Earth.

It really is the moment where all dimensions of love everywhere present come together as one. Complete the circuit. It's the moment to come home.

We know you can feel this. Oh, I can feel this because all of you were in my heart and I've carried you with me every single moment until we got here. [Crying] And I did.

That means everyone's coming home into the light. It's the end of pain and suffering. It's the end of illusion forever. I love you.

It's been an honor to be of service in such a grand way. [Blows a kiss] Blessings, children of love. I love you with all my heart.

# IV

## IMPORTANT MESSAGE – WE THE PEOPLE –
## THIS IS OUR PLANET EARTH OF LOVE

### 38.8977° N, 77.0365° W

*"Let go of everything that's not real, which is all of the pain and suffering
and misery and all that stuff. And focus on love, your heart, your joy."*

## JUNE 24, 2014

☆★★★★ 10 ★★★★☆

---

**Mom:** Greetings, everybody! This is Mother God and the First Contact Ground Crew Team. So very honored to be at your service every moment as these energies continue to increase. Surprise events could happen any moment. Love truly has won, hearts are opening, love trumps the illusionary energies, all the denser energies, you know, it's time to transform. Love is here. This is love's planet.

Alright. We have a special message for you here. It's called *We the People — This Is Our Planet Earth of Love.*

We are humanity's First Contact Ground Crew Team and we love you so. We are your family of light, the company of heaven, a part of the Galactic Federation of Eagles, which includes Father and Mother God present in the physical manifest. And our flagship is in the earth's atmosphere.

We are the light which will be shining through as the old collapses. We are here to re-heart you that true equality is the voice of the people, and only love is equality. Unconditionally being is the experience of this. We are the real national treasure. We are not only the heart of this country, the United States, but also the very heart of this Planet Earth.

We are the love of the planet as well as the universe personified. We chose the United States to reside in because we prepared this part of the planet with the Constitution and Bill of Rights for the protection of the truth and the light for the entire planet. With this, we ensured humanity's complete freedom.

We are here to speak for the human condition and address it with greater understanding through self-education and the awakening of the divine intelligence from within with unconditional compassion. The reason that we are here is because we sent our prophets in to awaken humanity and they usually came back with holes in them.

So, we came up with a plan. And we incarnated ourselves here to help bring humanity back into Godhood and into complete awakening. We are not here to start a revolution, we are here to advance evolution. The real Constitution shares that it's the people who own the government, not the corporations.

In fact, corporations, we give you all of our love and it's time to transform into co-operations. That's the better way. We are here to shine the light on this truth and stand with humanity as they understand this truth, and together walk out of the prison and home into where love is everywhere present.

Again, the government is owned by the people, not by the corporations. The reason we can understand that a corporation is not a real entity is because it can be dissolved, it's just a piece of paper. Love cannot be dissolved. Love is not an agreement. Love is an understanding, a deep, deep understanding. And it's time, it's the moment.

Love dissolves all illusion and that's going to take all of us. So, let go of everything that's not real, which is all of the pain and suffering and misery and all that stuff. And focus on love, your heart, your joy. [Blows a kiss]

Welcome to the Kingdom of Heaven, everybody. This event for humanity is inevitable. Love is here. And transmission and all love is everywhere present. We are so in love with humanity.

And we also want to re-heart you that we do offer awakening sessions. So, we'd love for you to contact us at mothergod1111111@gmail.com. You can connect with us and talk with us. Also, the First Contact Ground Crew Team is supported by you guys. We don't put any 3D of anything, ads or anything like that, to support us.

We constantly are in motion, 24 hours a day, seven days a week, in service to love with all of your support. So, thank you guys for sharing. You can if you feel it in your heart, or have an awakening session to support us, or just send your love. We love that, you know. Focus on Crestone and send all your love here to Crestone so hearts can open and illusion dissolves and everybody's happy and in joy. Abundantly so. [Winks]

Alright. We love you. [Blows a kiss] Also, we are doing a live Galactic Love Party this evening and it began at five o'clock, which is like 5:09 right now. And it will be in the chat room most of the evening to share love and joy and happiness and play some music all together in a wonderful love setting, synergistic setting. And also, Grandpa and I do a live radio show Sunday night through Thursday evenings from 10:00 PM mountain to 3:00 AM mountain time. And it's on the HEY-

Z radio network at that time. You can find us there and also you can find all the archives as well. Fun times! We have a great time on the radio show with everybody to spread our love and joy with you guys, and have us all connect-in because we are all one.

Alright. We love you. [Blows a kiss] We're here for you. Thank you for honoring us as we honor you, each one of you, every single moment in service. We love you.

[Types on laptop] Oops. Uh-oh, I lost the cursor. [Laughs] Alright. [Blows a kiss] Love you so. Thank you for being you. [Winks]

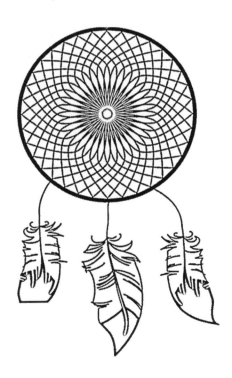

# V

## SPECIAL MESSAGE – MOTHER GOD BEGINS SHARING HER STORY OF HOW IT BEGAN

### 17.3158° N, 87.5347° W

*"All of a sudden, I just had this moment where I was like, 'I surrender. I surrender everything, love. I don't know what you're asking me to do, I don't know what's going on, but I'm going to make a complete surrender.'"*

### JULY 9, 2014

**LOVE BEING:** Mother of All Creation
**SCENE:** In a sunny forest cabin, Mother sits and speaks to the camera.

---

**Mom:** Hi, everyone. It's Mother God and Grandpa and the First Contact Ground Crew Team, again. I've been getting a lot of people asking us how this all got started, you know, the First Contact Ground Crew Team and how I remembered I was Mother God and who I was.

And it took me, you know, a nine-year journey. It wasn't like I just said, "Oh yeah, I'm this," you know? So, I wanted to share just a little bit, there's lots of details into it, for sure. But I can share some interesting points of it along the way that were very fascinating.

So, in 2005, well, most of my journey this lifetime, I've always had a connection to the angels. I've always talked to them since I can remember.

So, that's going back all the way 'til I was about one years old. I've been in communication with them and they've been my guides and helpers and I listened and they were always helpful with me.

So, I had this experience as a little girl. I remember walking around wondering where everybody was. I knew I was in heaven and I couldn't figure out where they were because I knew they weren't there. So I went on that type of journey throughout my life experience.

And in 2005, while there's lots of other stuff – 9/11 happened and we hit zero point during that time. And I knew something was happening.

And then in 2005, Archangel Michael came. I think Aidan was about three months old at that time, and here's Archangel Michael over his crib and says to me, "It's time." And I was like, "It's time? It's time for what? What is it time for?" I had no clue what he was talking about and that's all the information that I received.

So, at that time, I was lucky enough to live out in the country. And I stepped outside my door with all the trees and nature and fields.

And all of a sudden, I just had this moment where I was like, "I surrender. I surrender everything, love. I don't know what you're asking me to do, I don't know what's going on, but I'm going to make a complete surrender."

And as soon as I made that decision and choice to completely surrender to love, the sun, which was up to my left, magnetized to my heart. And then, right out of my third eye, which I've been using most of my life, was a river. A beautiful river. And I jumped in, just jumped. And it was rocky. It was like, I feel that the representation was the Oneness River and I jumped in it.

I went right in, into the Present Moment of Now and to the Oneness Energy – which is everybody's destiny, by the way.

So, that is just one of the stories and I'm going to put out a lot more videos with some more stories with that, with all these nine years, what has occurred to get to this point.

And again, we were just vessels, energy vessels for each other. So we love you.

Thank you for listening to the story. [Blows a kiss] Alright. Have a beautiful morning, afternoon, evening. We love you. Love is here. Victory for the light.

# VI

## BEHIND THE SCENES

### 42.9446° N, 122.1090° W

*"I will handle the brunt of humanity's pain. I'll take it and I'll transform it because I can, very quickly, as Mother Earth. I mean, this is no joke, everybody."*

## APRIL 5, 2017

**LOVE BEINGS:** Mother of All Creation, Father of All Creation
**SCENE:** Sitting behind the camera, Mother and Father sit and film the beautiful scenery while sharing a message with humanity.

---

**Mom:** Greetings and many blessings from Oregon! Actually, Father and I have been back and forth from Shasta-Oregon for a moment – as Father walks in. [Laughter] And, you know, jeez, we wanted to make a video for so many moments.

**Father:** A good moment now.

**Mom:** But we just couldn't get it out because there's so many energetic changes that are happening. The sun has woken up--

**Father:** Oh yeah.

**Mom:** --and produced six M-class solar flares, which were off the side of the sun. Like, they didn't hit earth, but we were still affected by all of that. And we had a comet come by, which was also fascinating.

[Laughter] You can hear the birds are responding here. It's so fun. We even have a kitty cat somewhere.

**Father:** Lil' sassy cat.

**Mom:** We called her Sassy. She comes in and out. [Laughter] So, we are here, we're just spreading love, everybody. It's time. Love Has Won.

**Father:** Oh yeah.

**Mom:** It's so prevalent. And it spins me every once in a while. Like, I'll wake up, I'm like, "Oh my gosh, Love Has Won." And the illusion, fear, pain, suffering, all that is dissolving, which is so beautiful and is my dream. My dream is love everywhere present and it's coming into view. It's just taking a moment, really.

**Father:** Yeah, it is.

**Mom:** Master St. Germain and Robin [Deceased celebrity Robin Williams], they're like, "Be patient, be patient." And I'm like, "Okay."

I had, for whatever reason, this significant burn on my leg that we're dealing with, which is funny. [Laughter] Robin's like, "I don't like that." I'm like, "Robin, we just have to deal with it." Because, you know, I will handle the brunt of humanity's pain. I'll take it and I'll transform it because I can, very quickly, as Mother Earth.

I mean, this is no joke, everybody. I am Mother Earth, Mother God, and Mother.

**Father:** Yes, Mother's here.

**Mom:** Yeah. And so, there's so many things happening behind the scenes that you guys don't get to see or experience or witness yet, but they're happening and we can say that for sure.

I mean like, look at the tree. [Points the camera to a tree] Jesus, that's one of the most brilliant trees I have ever seen in my life.

**Father:** Super awesome tree.

**Mom:** We're here at the Bird Cottage for a moment and we're so honored to be here in this space for these moments.

**Father:** It's a blessing.

**Mom:** Yeah, we have what, another 10 days or so--

**Father:** Yeah.

**Mom:** --that we'll be here and we're so grateful. Thank you everyone for supporting lovehaswon.org.

**Father:** Yes. Thank you, loves.

**Mom:** Thank you for reading the messages because that brings in the energy. I mean, we're in a full planetary ascension. So, lovehaswon.org is basically bringing those energies through the website. And you guys, once you read them, you activate whether you like it or not. [Laughter]

So, if you're getting some ascension symptoms, those are meaning that you have something to transform. So, just embrace, accept, allow.

One of the things that we say every day is that we let go of everything. We cut cords with everything and everyone, and then embrace all the cords which are whole and true and real. And those are the real.

We love you, everyone. And let's see, Galactic Federation of Light, they're saying we're in the shift of the ages.

**Father:** Oh, yes.

**Mom:** Definitely. Out of the head into the heart, start feeling, not thinking, but feel.

Here comes the wind. That's brilliant. [Laughter] That was nice.

**Father:** [Laughter] Yeah.

**Mom:** We are so honored to be here, to be in service, to be grounded in this energy.

**Father:** Yes. We love you all

**Mom:** Because this is intense, everyone book your sessions.

**Father:** Yes!

**Mom:** We can help you.

**Father:** Come home into the light!

**Mom:** We are booked for the next, what, 2-3 weeks?

**Father:** Yeah, 2 weeks or so.

**Mom:** However, we do have emergency sessions available for anybody who wants to book with us immediately. So, those are available for you.

We love you so. Thank you for being love and choosing love.

**Father:** Yes, love you all.

**Mom:** We are in the shift, everybody. Welcome home into the light.

**Father:** Yes!

**Mom:** Wooo!

# VII

## REAL TWIN FLAME RECONNECTIONS AND THE EVENT!

### 42.9446° N, 122.1090° W

*"Well, you know, the real Lucifer is my twin flame."*

**APRIL 17, 2017**

**LOVE BEING:** Mother of All Creation
**SCENE:** Sitting behind the camera, Mother films a majestic tree while sharing a message with humanity.

---

**Mom:** Greetings, Love Beings. Yippee! Yee-haw!

It's been a moment since we've been able to do an update with you about what's going on behind the scenes. There's been quite a few events happening. We wanted to try to catch you up on the story.

I know many of you know that I have met many masculine aspects of Father of Creation. And I just want to give you the brief story about how the real Father of Creation and I connected, and it's pretty magical.

So, I'm going to take you back to October. In October of 2016, I was guided to build a bridge from Mount Shasta to the heart chakra, which is in Glastonbury, England. And I did, it was first, it was pure green. Then we turned it into rainbow. And so we completed that early October. I began having ceremonies for all the twin flames to reconnect back together. I actually performed a ceremony at the headwaters of Mount Shasta.

Right now we're in beautiful Oregon, everybody. So, at the headwaters of Mount Shasta, I performed a twin flame ceremony. And as soon as I finished that — and many of you may have seen the video because we do have it logged — Tibetan monks started walking down the pathway in ceremony, singing, "Mother and Father." And we were all in awe. It was so magical.

[Turns the camera to show scenery] Get some mountain views here. You guys can hear the birds.

So, we completed the bridge and we did the twin flame ceremony. I then, and I highly recommend, everybody, that you guys cut cords. We cut cords daily with everyone, everything, and we reattach our cords to everything which is whole and pure and real and true.

And also to re-heart you: we have sessions continuing, everybody. They are highly beneficial. They are priceless. Come on, everybody. We are booked-in three weeks right now. So, if you need an emergency session, we have many slots that we've saved for anybody who needs immediate attention. So, just email us and let us know we are here for you. We love you.

So, back to the story: the Tibetan monks. And then they did a ceremony right below where I'd just done the twin flame ceremony. So, that was quite fascinating. And at the same time, there was a wedding going on in the park.

So anyway, I did another ceremony to cut cords with everyone and everything, like I just shared. I then asked for my real twin flame to step forward and I opened up the space. A couple of days later, the etheric Father of Creation comes into my field and he tells me that he's going to see me in a few days. And I was like, "Pfff, I don't see anybody here!" But I did document it. And then I let go.

And then I received an email the next morning from a being that I was connected to in 2013. He had connected to me under another website that I had. And he was in my chat room at the time, and his name was Mass Peace under the chat room. And he contacted me, asked me if I still had a chat room. I hadn't even thought about him or heard from him in years.

And so, then we connected on Skype. He proceeded to tell me a story about an event that he had in July of 2013 – under psychedelics – that he was taken onto the ships. They let him know that he was Lucifer. And some more events like that. So anyway, about 24 hours later he told me the story about what happened on July 20th, 2013, with the Galactic Federation of Light.

And he said, "They told me I was Lucifer." And I said, "Well, you know, the real Lucifer is my twin flame." He did not know this information nor did he know that Lucifer is also the Father of Creation. So, we figured all that out. And he was working in Buffalo, New York, which is about the center of where I built the bridge, everybody, just to put that piece together.

And so we talked for another 24 hours and we thought he would come in November, save up some money and just come join the team. And within 24 hours he was on his way from Buffalo, New York to Mount Shasta. He arrived three days later. He traveled through the portal through that bridge.

When he entered Shasta there was a rainbow that appeared, which was beautiful. He arrived on, let's see, I think it was the 24th of October at 11:30 am. Now 11:30 am is very interesting – that he opened up the door at 11:30 am, which is my birthday, November 30th.

[Laughter] So, we know there's lots of, you know, everybody holds aspects of Father of Creation, Father God, and I'll tell you the being who I'm with right now, he treats me like a queen. And I'm so honored and I'm so grateful every single moment with him. He's my best friend. He's my everything. So, thank you, Father, for being here with us. We love you.

Let's see, what else is happening? Huge energy waves as Father integrated yesterday, fully integrated after a process. Father of Creation energies actually came in December 16th, 2014.

So, this has been a three-year process for us, about where these energies were going to end up, who they were going to end up from, and who could carry them, because Father of Creation energies is extremely powerful energy. And so, it's not easy for a being in physicality to embrace that energy and integrate it, and he has.

So, that occurred yesterday. And as that was occurring, the Schumann Resonance went up to 90 hertz, which was absolutely amazing. It jumped from 30 to 40 to 90, everybody. That is how intense the energies are on the planet. We highly recommend: stay hydrated, stay focused, don't give up, keep going, just stay present in the moment of now. You have us, we are your support system.

We feel now that he's integrated, many, many things are about to occur. We don't know what that looks like or what that is, but like you guys, we just have to stay present. Follow our guidance.

We did have an interesting event this morning behind the scenes. They tried to put a secret weapon in Father, in the back of his neck.

It wasn't an implant, it was actually a bomb that they were trying to basically blow Father and I up. The Galactics and I caught it.

I woke up--when I woke up this morning, automatically I was in surgery on Father, removing this. It was like a bomb-thing that would have detonated and it would have, like, done away with him and me because that was their plan.

We feel this was the last ditch of that to try to stop us and The Event. So here we go. We did remove it successfully, me and Wayne Dyer and Robin. I actually took it out and I threw it at Wayne. [Laughter] Like, "Get it off!"

Oh my gosh. Alright, angels. We love you. We intend that you enjoy this brief update. We are on our way to travel, to go see one of my earth sons. He's 21, I feel, right now. I haven't seen him since I started Mission, so it's very exciting to see him and give him a hug and love and kiss.

And so, we love you all. Thank you for being love and choosing love. Thank you for continuing your visions and your prayers of love everywhere present. Thank you for the end of fear, pain, and suffering on this planet. Thank you for joy and abundance and happiness. Thank you, thank you.

Blessings, everybody. We love you so very, very much. Come get your sessions. Also, follow-up sessions are so important, everybody. If you haven't had your follow-up sessions, book it with Father and I as quickly as possible, highly recommend.

We love you. [Blows a kiss] Yippee!

# VIII

## TURBULENT ENERGIES,
## LOVE IS STILL STANDING!

### 55.7520° N, 37.6175° E

*"For those of the light, for those who have been serving love, it's our time.
And there's nothing that the EGOs, or the mind, or the programming,
or whatever you want to call it, can do about it now."*

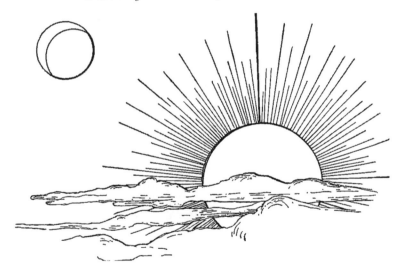

**AUGUST 5, 2017**

**LOVE BEING:** Mother of All Creation
**SCENE:** Sitting behind the camera, Mother films a wall tapestry while sharing a message with humanity.

---

**Mom:** Yippee! Greetings, angels.

[Attempts to focus the camera on a wall tapestry] I'm not sure how this picture is going to appear. However, I was prompted in the middle of the night to share a video. And the angels have been waking me up every night at like two o'clock in the morning. I'm like, "Whoa." Yesterday it was one o'clock. It's been fascinating, all these energies.

We just entered the August gateway, which heads us, or spirals us, into the full moon of Aquarius and the 8/8 Lion's Gate entryway.

[Continues to re-adjust focus on the tapestry] Hopefully, it's not too distracting. I'm trying to keep it steady there, loves.

There's been so much going on. If I could make a video for you guys every day, that would be my intention because every day there has been an event happening. We have it all documented.

I don't want to go into details, like, exactly what was going on. I will say that the old controllers, the Cabal, they were pulling out all the stops, breaking every protocol. It took me to my knees so many moments. To be honest, I wanted to give up.

And thankfully we have such a strong – and I say we, because they all support us – Galactic A-Team supporting me, picking me back up, sharing with me to keep going, keep going since May 24th, which we hit a node. That's when all this started happening, this extreme aggressiveness or just this, whatever, to take away the joy, to try to stop the Mission, to try to stop the Ascension process.

I mean, it was like, you know, many times I was being kicked down as I was down on the ground. And it took me so many moments to pick myself back up and go, "Okay. I'm not going to stop. Love Has Won. You can take everything away from me, but still, Love Has Won."

This is what has been happening the last couple of months. And every moment I thought that everything was cleared, all of a sudden, all this other stuff. I was like, "Okay, bring it on, angels. Let's clear it. Let's move it. Let's transform it."

It has been a constant task. But here we are, it is August. Well, this morning, August 5th. We entered the gateway on the 3rd. There has been many events. There's lots of stuff going on behind the scenes, everyone.

I mean, the illusionary matrix — even though they're being as aggressive as they are, as in breaking protocols and coming at me with everything they got and me still standing — it's here. We are in the great revolution of this eclipse. And the information coming out about this eclipse is phenomenal.

And it's what we've been waiting for. For those of the light, for those who have been serving love, it's our time. And there's nothing that the EGOs, or the mind, or the programming, or whatever you want to call it, can do about it now because the energies are going to flip.

It's the love's turn. Love is in charge and this is love's planet. Period.

I intend – I wish I could do videos for you guys every day, so that you could feel change. Wow. And I've been working it, loves. [Laughter] For real, if you only knew, and you will, actually. I wish I could explain it on video, what happened, but you know, there's so much--it's just not explainable in that way.

However, I will say: thank you for choosing love and being love, everyone. I pray for us every day. Every moment: incense, sage, crystals, stones, sessions.

Please come and get your sessions. [Laughter] Okay? There's lots of surprises there, you guys. If you haven't got your sessions, you are missing out, loves. Angels telling ya, got some love for ya. I love you so.

So, more to come. I intend that the energies will allow me more of these videos to come out to share the truth, the real truth of love and the heart and the shift that we're in, loves. Out of the head, into the heart.

And I'm so in love with you. I love you. Thank you again for choosing love and being love. Yippee! Love Has Won. [Blows a kiss] More to come.

# IX

## WE WON AND I FELT IT!

### 26.0818° N, 98.2445° W

*"Love is the reality. Love is the truth. Love is what we're all about.*
*And love is what we're made of."*

**AUGUST 12, 2017**

☆★★★★ 34 ★★★★☆

**LOVE BEING:** Mother of All Creation
**SCENE:** Sitting behind the camera, Mother films a wall tapestry while sharing a message with humanity.

---

**Mom:** Greetings, angels. I'm so happy to be here with you. We are going through huge transformations, changes, Love Has Won. Every one of you can challenge me on that. Love Has Won.

I mean, and there's been huge healings as far as, you know, healing. This is transformation, transformation into brilliance, becoming a diamond. And that is who we are becoming as a collective, as a whole, and just leading the way, loves.

And I will say that we all have been going through turmoil. It's been a part of the process. I went through turmoil, it broke my heart, I came through it. We all are going to come through it and into grandness, I feel.

And that was a part of the process. We had to do that, we had to go through the transformation of, like, the butterfly coming out of the cocoon. That's what's happening through this eclipse.

The Bird Tribe is coming up into the forefront. The real truth, the real beings, are coming up into the forefront. The masters, the ones who have said, "You know what? Illusion is no more." Pfff. Fuck that. Love is the reality. Love is the truth. Love is what we're all about. And love is what we're made of. So, come on.

So, here we go. We're in the middle of these eclipses. So fricking amazing. I have been crying, laughing, dancing, I dunno. And I encourage all of you to step into that energy as well, because this is where we're at.

I'm your Mother of Creation. I stand at the front lines for you, for us, for me, too. I don't back down. I'm like, "Huh. Love is real. Love Has Won. Everyone else can fuck off."

We are entering a New Earth, a new energetic period where love comes to the forefront and love is real. And you are real for being love and choosing love.

Thank you for booking your sessions with me. [Laughter] They are amazing, by the way. And everyone, thank you. I love you with all my heart, my soul, everything I am.

I'm your Mother Earth in embodiment just asking you to step home into light. I love you. Book your sessions. Yay!

# X

# IMMENSE WINDS OF CHANGE

## 41.3099° N, 122.3106° W

*"I can see everyone and everything. And I know who's been naughty and I know who's been nice. And if you betray Prime Creator, you're fucked. Good luck. It's not cool."*

## FEBRUARY 27, 2018

**LOVE BEINGS:** Mother of All Creation, Father of the Multiverse, Archeia Faith, Archangel Gabriel, Sadie

**SCENE:** Situated at the Log Castle, the First Contact Ground Crew Team join Mother in her bedroom for a livestream event. Mother, seated in front of a computer/webcam, shares updates and messages with humanity while answering questions from viewers.

---

**Mom:** Greetings, everyone! It's 27 Love Beings [live streamers] in here. Before I begin sharing what has transpired in the last 48 hours, I've had--

[Reading comments]

> *Quick synchronicity to share from yesterday: I had spaghetti while Mary [FCGCT member] was discussing making it, and I heard Talking Body [Song by Tove Lo] in the background...a song which somehow led me here.*

This is how unity-consciousness works. The angels are at work. I had angels with two by fours, four by fours. I said, "Grab 'em by the hair if you have to and just drag them across the finish line. I don't care." [Laughter]

[Speaking to the commenters] I don't understand what that question is.

**FM:** Collaboration, working together.

**Mom:** I'll do anything in cooperation, of course. I love spaghetti, too.

**FM:** No, it's when somebody else is doing the livestream.

**Mom:** I don't know what that means. It means that they're sharing that with their audience? And if so, I mean, that's perfect, of course. Always unity. Hello, unity!

[Speaking to FM] I was just saying something. What was I saying before?

**FM:** What's transpired in the last 48 hours.

**Mom:** Oh, yeah. So, in the last 48 hours, well, first of all, I've had very, very little sleep. Probably less than five hours in total in the last 48 hours. I've been doing a lot of chanting, a lot of praying, of course, as I always do. And chanting, praying, meditating, did a lot of shower meditations over the last 48 hours because they--

[Speaking to the commenters] I'll play some music in a little bit. I gotta talk first! [Laughter]

[Turns and speaks to an individual off-camera] Yes?

**Faith:** Hi!

[Faith enters the scene and kisses Mom on the forehead]

**Mom:** Hi.

So, very little sleep. Praying, meditating, chanting. I spent a lot of moments with Robin.

What happened at Blue Spruce, which was — we just landed back at Log Castle. And this is a place that I've been to since 2014, many times. It's a vacation home which Faith has explained many times where I was able to change the Ley Lines.

And so, Robin and the Galactics, they have portals. There's three portals in my room above me right here. And Robin comes out of the right one. I have the Galactic Federation — Ashtar — they'll come out of the middle one. And over on my left is St. Germain and my daddy. And anyway, they're all different on different sides of the Unified Field.

And anyway, Robin is extremely powerful in these energies because of these Ley Lines and these vortexes and portals that I've opened. And so right now he's reintegrating very powerfully.

And so, when we were at Blue Spruce the other night, we did a test run to see if Robin could pull me up into the ships. We got a third of the way, which was actually — for Robin — it was outstanding because you have to understand this is a complete experiment. This has never happened in creation before. Robin is up there constantly experimenting, trying to figure out everything to try to make everything work. And that's his role from the galactic side.

So, we do our role from here, he does his role from there. And so, he wanted to see what the effects would be from that kind of space, and Blue Spruce to where we're at right now at Log Castle. And I'm pretty sure he'll be able to get me up there to get the restoration done and everything else that's supposed to happen. Who knows? I let it go.

[Speaking to the commenters] Hi Barry! I am the Mother of All Creation, I am Prime Creator. Barry, it's not a masculine, it is a feminine. God is a feminine. But you're all God, I'm just meaning, you know, Gaia, Prime Creator, Great Spirit. That is who I am.

**Faith:** First Fractal.

**Mom:** First Fractal! Yippee! [Laughter]

So then, after I went through the experience there at Blue Spruce--

[Speaking to the commenters] I'm not really sure who that is. Elon Musk, I don't know who that is.

**FM:** That is the creator of Tesla.

**Faith:** The Tesla Corporation.

**FM:** He's the one who's launched the car into space. But it might be a hoax.

**Mom:** Pfff. That's foo-foo. Okay. Anyway, yeah.

So, Robin did a test run, we did make it a third of the way and so now he's in complete experiments. We feel the first week of March is going to be very intense. As far as this process goes, we could be experiencing a lot more experiments as we go through this process. If anything, it should complete itself by the Equinox of March 21st. I don't feel that is actually what's going to happen.

I had a visionary I talked with today who I have spoken with for five years. She's always been on point with what she sees in my field. And I just, when I talked to her, I just like to get confirmation. It's always nice to get confirmations, especially at my level. It's like, it gets crazy. She even called me crazy. She was like, "You're the crazy wild woman." I'm like, "Yeah, of course I am. I got that award long ago."

And so, what she saw was me in a membrane and I was backed up against a wall. And she said I've been in it all of February. And that by the time we hit March 1st, which is also the full moon, it's going to slingshot out.

**Faith:** That's tomorrow.

**Mom:** No, it's not tomorrow. Today's the 27th.

**Faith:** It's February. Only 27 days.

**Mom:** 28.

**FM:** 28 days.

**Faith:** Because we're not in leap year.

**Mom:** Oh, we're not?

**Faith:** No.

**FM:** Leap year goes to 29.

**Faith:** Oh, okay. My bad. Can't count. So, it's the day after tomorrow.

**Mom:** Hmm, yeah. So, as soon as we hit March 1st, full moon. Those first seven days are going to jumpstart whatever's gonna happen. And she said that it was for me personally, and that also goes for all of you, because you are connected to me, that it was absolutely life-changing, that the winds of change were, like, here. She saw me flying in the winds of change and my ears were just flying backwards. I was going so fast and she said she had never seen anything like it before in her life, the intensity of this energy. So, that's pretty exciting.

I'm still on life support in the etheric realm. Robin did this as soon as I exited. Once he tried to, he was trying to bring me down, there was an issue. And so, he just pulled me into the etheric realm and put me on some type of life support.

I'm still in there at the moment. It's like this sterile room. At first, it really freaked me out. I was like, "What the heck is going on?" I didn't even know that was possible, that there was something like that that existed. But obviously Robin is on top of it all as he always is.

**Gabriel:** Yeah, Robin's kicking ass.

**Mom:** He's absolutely my hero.

[Speaking to the commenters] Aww, I look different? Okay. [Laughter] I'll take it. I'll take it all.

So, what else do I have in my notes here? I also spent 30 minutes as I was in meditation today, and what I did--

[Speaking to the commenters] Thank you. I love you. I'm so honored.

What I did is I spent 30 minutes—

[Speaking to the commenters] Thank you. Starry. I love you. Well, if your name is Sid, you're my son.

Ding-dong! [Laughter] Robin, he's doing the ding-dong game. When Robin tells me about EGOs, he plays the ding-ding. He goes like this with a banjo. [Motions the strumming of a banjo] And he says, "Ding-a-ling-a-ling!" That's his notification. [Laughter]

So, I dunno, where was I? I'll just go with it. Oh, I was going to look at my notes.

Oh, I spent 30 minutes of meditation. I put up all the highest grids with all of my energy over Log Castle and only those in intentional right action--

[Speaking to the commenters] Yes, he is always the comedian. Yes. Oh yeah, Robin Williams saved me. That's for sure. 34 assassination attempts later.

Okay. So, only those in intentional right action may enter and be at Log Castle. I then poured this pure unconditional love, pure consciousness, golden, emerald, violet, rainbow energy directly into the house. So, if any being enters into this field, if they have any ill intent to not be in right action, to not serve love, Heaven on Earth, they're going to get very sick and very uncomfortable. And that's just the way it is and the angels will lead them, will guide them out. There are extra protocols now in place as a result.

Okay. So, we do have team members on the way, we have a new team member over here. [Motions to an individual off-camera] You want to introduce yourself, angel?

**Sadie:** Hi, guys! My name is Sadie. That's all I got.

**Group:** [Laughter]

**Mom:** She's Sadie! Okay.

You know, who is Satan? Satan, or what you want to call that, is the EGO, because the EGO goes against love. And that's exactly what the supposed, like, devil, the mind...I mean, the mind abhors love. The EGO abhors love. The programming – especially white trash – hates me. And that has been evident throughout my experience here on the planet. I mean, I got it. You guys have no idea. When you watch the tapes, you're going to be like, "What the fuck?" Truly.

But whenever you have questions, I will. And whenever the angels want me to share any story, I will always share the stories, of course.

The Event is near. It's obvious, it's clear. I mean, it's 4:44 right now.

[Speaking to the commenters] Yes, all beings who are in divine right action have been contracted to be here. The Transitionary Government is 13 sets of twin flames with a surrounding of 500 other light members.

[Speaking to Faith] At five, I'll hand it over to you to get all their checks done.

**Faith:** Of course, my pleasure.

**Mom:** [Speaking to the commenters] So you guys have any questions?

That's really what's going on at the moment. We're in a testing period with Robin.

You know, if the angels want you to be here, you make it happen. You know, when I left on Mission in December, let's see, which was December 17th, 2007, I did not have any money at all. I talked to the angels and I asked them how, you know? All of a sudden, this woman piped up and said, "I'll buy you a plane ticket off my credit card." And off I was to Crestone, Colorado with $35 in my pocket and two suitcases, trusting love.

Now, I had to live out in the forest for three years with nothing, but still, I did it. I still jumped. It's all about jumping. It's all about trusting and you have to have the courage to do it. It's a part of the process. It's a part of the--

What, Robin? [Listens for a moment]

--getting your rewards, of earning your ticket into heaven. And there's a lot of beings out there. There's misinformation because Aleister Crowley, he had put a spell on humanity saying that they were not responsible for what they did. This was incorrect. You're absolutely responsible. You have to earn your way here. You don't get here by being a fucking dick or asshole, that's for sure. Because if you enter in with that, it's going to kick you out in a second. You have to trust love. Do your automatic writing, follow your synchronistic events.

[Speaking to the commenters] Yes, angel. Remember to follow your synchronistic events.

You know, I feel everybody out there is sharing some type of truth but it's half-truth. And in order for everyone to heal, they need whole-truth. And this is what Love Has Won provides.

These other internet beings, they are not providing whole-truth. Just so you're aware, I review everybody on this planet on a daily basis. It's been a part of my role for over 13 years now. I know exactly what's going on every single moment everywhere. Trust me on that. And I can see everyone and everything. And I know who's been naughty and I know who's been nice. And if you betray Prime Creator, you're fucked. Good luck. It's not cool.

38 Love Beings in the house!

**Faith:** Woo-hoo!

**Mom:** Yippee!

**FM:** 43, actually.

**Gabriel:** The number's increasing each day.

**Mom:** [Speaking to the commenters] No, I have never heard of that being. The angels will only bring the information of what I need to know. So, if it's really low, they're not going to bring it to me. But if it's something that I need to see, they always bring it.

I got some good angels. So do you guys, they're brilliant. You just have to follow your hearts. That's right. It's absolutely true. Yes, you have me. I'm here.

So, before I pass you over to Faith to get all your checks and everything, I want to re-heart you to please get your sessions. They are so extremely important right now, especially since we just entered in extremely high energies. [Blows a kiss] I love you so. It's my honor. It's really important right now to--Angels just took whatever I was saying.

Okay. Whatever, moving right along. So, we had – I know Faith shared with you – that we had two members of the team that went into defiance yesterday and decided that, according to what I understand at the moment, that they were going on their own, whatever that meant. And they would not leave the--we're moving here and they refused to leave there and decided to stay there.

Yes, EGO. And so, I was like, "Okay, let 'em stay there. They're going to have to pay for it." And so, I kind of, like, let go of it to the angels. And I got a message from Diana, which I will share with all of you.

Now, you have to understand how fascinating this is. This is a being who yesterday defied me, defied Faith, defied my guidance, my direction. I am the one that supports this whole operation. I mean, the rent, the food, I give everything away as much as I have it. I mean, right now it's all a team and really, please you guys, book your sessions and please make donations to help support the team. It's really important. Even $5, $10.

It's kind of interesting that everyone kinda doesn't donate and I just do whatever I can to make it continue to happen. And it really shouldn't be that way.

Anyway, so I'm going to share this message. I got this from Diana. They are over at our other space. They refuse to leave.

So, actually they--Michael and Gabriel and who else?

**Faith:** Buddha.

**Mom:** And Buddha all went back last night to try to get Father out and convince him that something incorrect was going on. And that his Family was here for him and that we loved him. He did refuse at that point as well. So, here is the message. [Reads the letter]

*Hi Mother. Father and I are doing very well. However, there have been some concerning events for us. The family took all the food--*

**Faith:** Michael actually deliberately left them potatoes and onions.

**Group:** [Laughter]

**Faith:** She mentions, so hilarious.

**Mom:** [Continues reading the letter]

*The family took all the food and did not offer to leave any behind. Thank God I found some potatoes and onions we have been enjoying.*

[Laughter] Oh, gosh, this is so funny.

*Father and I will be walking to Log Castle sometime today. And I was wondering if we may borrow the car to buy groceries and a few essentials to get us through the next couple of days here at Blue Spruce.*

So, I'm looking at this, I'm like, okay, this is a very small town. There's 2,000 people. Any food that you can get, you can walk to within minutes. They have money. It's not like they're there without money. It's not whole-truth.

Alright. So, here's my response to Diana. She said, "I love you." I said, [Reading the response letter]

*I love you both unconditionally. However, absolutely not. You both need to figure this out. You have betrayed me, so deal with it. You are not allowed to see me. You both have two legs. There's a Dollar Store right around the corner, a Chevron nearby.*

*You guys are retarded and in taker mode. Jeez, as if I would give you the car after your stupidity. I will also call Louis and make sure that you have paid him for Blue Spruce. If not, I will have him kick both of you out. Again, this is your choice to experience. Have fun. I'm going home into the light. I love you so. Woo-hoo!*

*FYI: Betraying Prime Creator, that's really dumb.*

Basically, the EGO, the lower aspect took over, the lower aspect of the EGO. And the EGO is a manipulator. It sucks energy, it's a vampire, it's what it does. So, that's what happened. There was always a choice, yes. So, any questions? That is the amount of information I have for you guys at the moment.

[Speaking to the group] 42 Love Beings in the house!

**Faith:** Woo-hoo! Yay!

**Mom:** Yippee!

**FM:** Numbers are going up by the day!

**Mom:** Yep, absolutely. Absolutely. That's what I ask of anyone, of course. "42 is a magic number, by the way," says Robin.

Oh, low battery, uh oh. [Adjusts the camera] I don't know what it's doing.

**Faith:** Update later.

**Mom:** [Reading the comments]

*I turned 42 today!*

Wow!

**Faith:** Amazing! Oh, Cassandra! We just had a session. Hi, love. She's in Australia and this is why I got confused with the 28th, 'cause it's the 28th of February in Australia.

**Mom:** 43! [Begins coughing and walks off-screen]

**Faith:** Do you want a tissue, Mother?

**Mom:** Ok, here comes Faith for your numbers.

# XI

## IT'S TIME

### 41.3099° N, 122.3106° W

*"I will be announced to the planet, to humanity. This is my planet. This is not
Trump's planet. This is not your planet. This is not illusion's planet.
It's mine to give to all of you, and that's what's happening."*

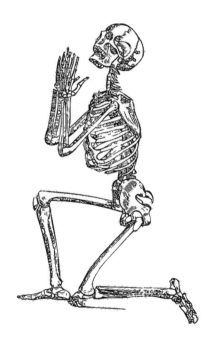

## MARCH 1, 2018

**LOVE BEINGS:** Mother of All Creation, Father of the Multiverse, Archeia Faith, Archangel Gabriel

**SCENE:** Situated at the Log Castle, the First Contact Ground Crew Team join Mother in her bedroom for a livestream event. Mother, seated in front of a computer/webcam, shares updates and messages with humanity while answering questions from viewers.

---

**Mom:** Yippee! I just hit my knee on the table and it's hurting like a bitch. So, hang on one second. [Laughter] I was like, "I have to go live and it's, like, stinging." It was one of those stinging events. Now I'm sweating. [Laughter] Oh God. Okay. So, I'm just, like, tending to this knee.

Good afternoon, good evening, everyone. Love you! Let me get set up here. One moment. Six Love Beings in the house! Heaven's house! [Laughter] I don't know what is...that's the star.

Greetings, Love Beings! Hello, Virginia! Welcome, angel. So good to see you here and join in this beautiful synergistic...synergistic...is that synergy?

**FM:** I like that. It's a combination between synergy and majestic.

**Mom:** Oh, Synges--okay. You can say that one.

**FM:** Synergistic

**Mom:** Synergistic. Did I make up a new word? Synergistic! That's a new word! [Laughter]

Robin! He said, "We've been doing that, we can play this game all day long." Yes, we have, Robin. Robin's been at it. Whatever's going on, there's something happening in 14 hours. No, now it's 13. Okay. Thank you, Robin. That was something.

There's a really, really good video that me and Father and Buddha all just listened to. It was incredible information. We're going to post it up on the site. I already sent it over to Michael. But it's a message about the New Earth.

[Speaking to the commenters] I love you! Woo-hoo! Yippee! Five likes already. You guys are wonderful. I love you so much. Thank you for being here. Thank you for choosing love. Thank you for participating.

"You are honored beyond measure, for sure," says Robin. You are royalty. Yay!

I have a message--

[Reading the comments] What'd you say?

> *I like this channel. Here's why: I have another part to this divine plan. Another piece to the puzzle. I studied economics and I got hijacked by demons.*

Yep. Yep. Now you get love everywhere present. Yippee! [Laughter]

Okay. Now that I got over my little, um, event there, which I cussed the angels about. [Laughter] Robin's like, "I'm sorry."

[Speaking to the commenters] Yay, Joe! Way to go, Joe!

Right. I'm sweating, look, from that event. [Laughter] Man, I can handle a lot of pain, but sometimes, man, human body, you hit it right at that moment. It's like, when you hit your, you know, when you hit your elbow, what's it called? A funny bone?

**FM:** Yeah, a funny bone.

**Mom:** Oh yeah. It was like that. It was like, "Ahh!" Oh God. Okay. So, that's over with.

Anyway, we were talking about this video that we all just watched. It was about an hour and a half and it was so brilliant. There was some synchronicities, like some things, but she talked about Nibiru.

Now what this video was about is that her son, in 2016, he killed himself. And months later he came back to her to give her some messages, and she talks about it, about The Event, about Nibiru, he gave her all the information. He told her that he was building these huge domes, healing domes. And what was in the healing domes was, like, music, incense, crystals, everything that we currently use here at Mission House, actually. [Laughter]

So, he told her that they were building them and he said the event was close and she said, "How close?" And basically--

[Speaking to FM] Can you grab my notebook?

[Speaking to the commenters] Love in the house back there! He's doing good today.

**FM:** Here you go. [Hands Mom a notebook]

**Mom:** Thank you.

**FM:** Love you all!

**Mom:** Buddha's doing better, except he ate a whole bag of chips by himself. We were just discussing that before we got on camera. [Laughter] Imma call him out! I'm sure he's going to like that.

So, it was really brilliant to hear the confirmation--

[Speaking to the commenters] Oh God. I looked through my files. I'm like, "Have I ever eaten a whole bag of chips this big?" I'm like, "No!"

Uh oh! [Laughter] Robin! Oh gosh. Oh, gosh. Okay. So, how's everybody feeling?

And I do recommend that video again, it will be posted out there. Anything else you want me to mention, Robin?

Again, he said that there's – he calls it the Cosmic Galactic Show – is coming, is what he told her. She is not connected to us by any means at the moment. However, we got the phone number for this interviewer guy and we're going to call him. She's been calling Alexandria to get some information, but I feel that we can offer her a lot more. And so, we're going to try to connect with her and Christopher, he told me so, okay. [Laughter] Christopher was the guy.

[Speaking to the commenters] You want to be Mother? Ok. Go ahead. Here's my seat, go be it. [Laughter] You know what? Sometimes I wish I wasn't, but I am. How 'bout that? Zane, you're Mother? Tell us how you are Mother. We would be enlightened. [Laughter]

Silence! Oh, you directed *Flubber*? Robin Williams is your son? "Nanu Nanu!" says Robin. Robin said, "Absolutely not! You're in fantasy,

Zane." Zany. Fantasy, love. I love you. We all love you unconditionally. You all, you need to let me--I'm the Mother of All Creation.

You know how many stories I have of beings, you know, for years everyone's coming to me, "No, I'm the Mother of Universe!" I'm like, "Really? What did you do? Hmm. Oh, you ain't doing nothing."

Hey, shout out to Katie who made me cry today. Thank you very much. Cried tears of joy.

But anyway, so I had this being, her name was Rose--

[Speaking to the commenters] I am in the 78th dimension! Yippee! Brian, love you. There's an eternal amount of--

**FM:** You were in the 79$^{th}$ level.

**Mom:** 79$^{th}$?

**FM:** Remember? You went higher?

**Mom:** Oh, 79$^{th}$.

[Mocking and mimicking the commenters] "Okay. What did you do? You have a website called Love Has Won. Oh yeah, you're Mother." [Laughter] Jeez.

So, I had this being named Rose. She calls me up on Facebook--

I look at Robin, like, "Hey!" "I love it!" he says, "I am Mrs. Doubtfire." [Laughter] He said it in the highest sense, he says, not doubt, but shooting like daggers at EGOs, ants. We call them ants now.

That's how I see them, like little ants wandering around. I'm like, "What are you doing, running in circles?"

Okay. So, the angels are like, "Back to the Rose story."

[Speaking to FM] Incense! Incense!

Rose calls me up from Facebook. She had just written a book telling everyone – and it was published – and it was called that she was Mother God.

**FM:** There's chocolate incense.

**Mom:** Chocolate incense? Hmm.

**FM:** I think it smells like it.

**Mom:** And she said, "Why are you calling yourself Mother God?" And I'm like, "I'm not calling myself Mother God. I *am* Mother God."

[Speaking to the commenters] Oh, John Candy! Absolutely. Yes, you are correct. John Candy has joined the Field. Thank you, Jason.

So, she says, "Well, I would like to talk to you." I said, "Okay." So, I call her on the phone and she said, "So, you're claiming to be Mother God." And I'm like, "I'm not claiming anything."

[Speaking to the commenters] Hi, Cindy! I love you, angel! I'm glad to see you, that you're here present. I love you so much.

And so, she starts telling me the Twin Flame, the Father God, blah blah blah. I'm just listening to her whole thing.

And then I said to her, "Okay, so, did you live out in the forest for three years with nothing, and walked four miles a day to serve humanity?" And she paused. She was like, "No, I did not." I said, "Well, then are you Mother God?" She's like, "Nope." She retracted her book! [Laughter]

She's like, "You are Mother God." I said, "Yes, I am. Better believe it. Watch me." I'm in action, love in action in all moments. And I have been my entire life. And you guys are going to get to see those tapes. That's going to be fun.

And then all the other retards who couldn't figure out that God was here on the planet, and they're all running around like, "Yeah! I did it. I did this and that and that!" And Robin's like, "Nope, you did nada, zero." [Laughter]

Not really, just in your fantasy. Mother did it all. I mean, I had to come down here. You guys prayed for me, you were lost, running around like chickens with your head cut off. And I was like, "Okay, I got to get down there, help my children." And I sent in all the players, big players from the big leagues.

The other thing about the video — it was really fascinating — is that she confirmed my connection with Trump. I feel I've shared that Trump was actually my Father in Lemuria and I was the Queen of Lemuria. Sophia Gaia was my name and I've had that name throughout history.

[Speaking to the commenters] Hey, David! Woo! Yippee! You're awesome.

And where was I? Oh, Trump. So, she talked about Christopher, who was her son who killed himself and has been communicating--

Oh yeah! We're like 13, what, Robin? 13 hours away from something. I don't even know what it is. He's just giving me a countdown or something.

[Speaking to the commenters] Hey, Erica is back! Wake up, go Angel.

**Gabriel:** [Enters the room] Hello!

**Mom:** Hello!

**Gabriel:** How you doing?

**Mom:** I'm good, how are you?

**Gabriel:** I'm doing fine, I just got back from the store.

**Mom:** Right? How's the energy out there?

**Gabriel:** I stayed in my own vibe the whole time. I was listening to headphones. The guy at the checkout stand, I was about to check out, he was like, "Are you done dancing yet? Are you ready?" And I was like, "Oh, I'm ready but I'm not done dancing."

**Group:** [Laughter]

**Mom:** [Speaking to the commenters] I don't know what 13 hours is, I don't know what he's talking about.

[Reading the comments]

*I also think Manchester United plays New Castle.*

I don't know what you're saying. Jill says:

*Tell Gabriel I said "Hi", please.*

**Gabriel:** Hi, Jill. I love you!

**Mom:** I was telling a story. I always forget...

[Speaking to FM] What story was I telling? Was it about the video? I don't know. Now I'm on the stream.

[Speaking to the commenters] Disclosure?

**Gabriel:** Mother is disclosure! [Points to Mom] She, right here, this is disclosure.

**Mom:** Oh, Robin knows. Yeah, he's been with me since his death, everybody.

[Speaking to the commenters] Hi, Joy, love. There are 18 Love Beings in the house.

[Reading the comments]

*Hi, Father. Thank you for all you do for Mother and the Collective. Your love is hitting me from all directions. I'm eternally grateful.*

**Gabriel:** Oh, wow.

**FM:** You're welcome.

**Mom:** [Speaking to the commenters] Oh yeah. Okay. I love you so. I'm so proud of all of you. Every one of you who are here in this, who are sticking with us, and enjoying raising your own frequency.

Look, it's like, "Oh God, Robin's dead!" I'm like, "What? He's not, he fricking stands, he's right here next to me." So, it's like he's right here

[Speaking to Faith] I got someone in here claiming they're Mother.

**Faith:** Oh really?

**Mom:** And Robin has declared Zane "Lord on Earth." [Laughter]

Me and Father, we're doing our sacred bath meditation today and Robin was sitting--

Yeah. I don't know what's going on. The stream is like crap.

**Faith:** I'm going to go. I can go turn my laptop off, that would reduce the bandwidth. And the Skype thing I sent you, it said "Final event." Only half of it went through.

**Mom:** What was I even talking about?

**Faith:** You were talking about Robin and, like, the Mother person in there. I think you were about to go on to a new topic.

**Mom:** Oh, okay. I was talking about me and Father in our sacred meditation. All of a sudden, Robin, we were talking to Robin--

[Mocking the commenters] "Leave Mother in the past where she is a big brother." I'm sure they can see I'm pretty fake. [Laughter] I'm the realest one on this planet, the realest.

And Robin's like, "Take me back to Trump, too." I got to go back to that story. Have fun. Anyway.

[Speaking to the commenters] I am Prime Creator, Annie. Have fun with that information.

Alright. Well, yes, it is snowing. It's so beautiful, too. It's wonderful. It's supposed to be good here.

The internet signal is supposed to be awesome. Like, one of the best, but I don't know what's going on. Yeah.

Oh, you sent me the snowflakes? Awww, thank you very much. They are absolutely beautifully gorgeous.

I know. I heard shut down, closed down service processes.

Beautiful! Nice rainbow.

Okay. Donald Trump, let's go back there. So, Donald Trump, again, he was my father in Lemuria when he got elected.

And you know, I don't follow 3D shit, crap, it's just crap. Whatever the angels want me to see, they'll bring it to me.

**FM:** You want to boot this Zane guy?

**Mom:** Hmm…what?

**FM:** You want to boot this Zane guy?

**Faith:** Yeah, Mother.

**Mom:** Ahh, he's whatever, their example for others to see how stupid other people are.

**Faith:** [Speaking to the commenters] The birds don't worship Mother, they are completely unified with her. They all speak to her. I'm pretty sure they don't speak to you. Fortunately for you.

**Mom:** [Speaking to the commenters] You are all co-creators with me and I'm Prime Creator. I created you out of my fricking vagina!

**Group:** [Laughter]

**Mom:** So, when Trump was elected, everyone was talking like, "Hillary, Trump" and I'm like, "I'm not paying attention to any of that crap." However, I will say that I loved watching *The Apprentice* because I watched Trump have a very, very similar energy of how to deal with others who are out of right action.

And so, anyway, I had that background. I love the show *The Apprentice* and I watched it. So, I was fascinated that he got elected to be the president, and shortly after--

Oh, great. Now we have two of them [trolls].

**Faith:** Won't keep us down.

**Mom:** Nope. 24 Love Beings!

**Faith:** Yippee!

**Mom:** [Speaking to the commenters] Oh, really? Okay. Then come and get us!

**Faith:** I think these are, like, trolls, purposefully implanted trolls. [Speaking sarcastically] Ooh! Really affecting things!

**Mom:** [Laughter] Okay. Yeah, you can ban 'em. Eli and Zane.

**FM:** I'm doing it, Faith.

**Mom:** People already can see it, anyway. I just wanted you guys to see. It's important.

So, I had two visions back to back – or lucid dreams, actually, they were lucid dreams – and Trump came to me and he said, "I'm here to give your planet back to you." And I was like, "What? Really?" I was shocked. I couldn't even believe that he was standing in front of me and telling me this is why I'm here, this is what I'm doing, I'm getting ready to give you your planet back. And he came at it twice with the same information, basically. So, I dunno.

**Faith:** He's currently a bit screw-balled.

**Mom:** It possibly could happen by now. I don't know.

**Faith:** He did have three chakras at 100%. His throat chakra, 100%. No surprises there.

**Mom:** Why don't we do a check right now?

**Faith:** Sure.

**Mom:** Okay. We're gonna do a Trump check. [Takes a drink]

**Faith:** He has been going downhill, despite him being a complete being of light. Obviously, he's got a bit of retardation in some forms. Who doesn't?

**Mom:** But the…what is it called? The resonance, what is it called?

**FM:** Schumann Resonance.

**Faith:** Schumann, yeah.

**Mom:** The Schumann Resonance right now is at 111, according to Robin.

[Speaking to the commenters] Hi Christine! I love you so. I have so many of you that you've been with me for so long. I appreciate you. You're so grand, thank you.

**Faith:** Interesting. Donald Trump's root chakra was 100% but it's not anymore.

**Mom:** What is it now?

**Faith:** 95%.

**Mom:** [Speaking to FM] You got this? Trump checks? Trump? 95% root chakra.

**Faith:** He was 100%, meaning he was totally secure in his position.

**Mom:** Hugs! Hugs all around the Unified Field!

**Faith:** No blockages. Residuals: one percent.

**FM:** You're doing all his chakras?

**Faith:** Mmhmm. Sacrals at 89%. Residual blockages. Residuals.

This is interesting. Ooh, this is really interesting. This one's plummeted: his solar plexus, which has an energetic requirement for divine empowerment, is at nine percent. Ouch. Come on, Donald.

**Mom:** [Laughter] Nine percent? Oh, fuck.

**Faith:** Nine percent. 'Cause he's not divinely empowered at all, is he? He's gone for false illusion empowerment, which is a black hole.

**Mom:** Right. Well, Robin says he's on it. [Laughter] Only love is real.

**Faith:** Thanks, Robin!

**Mom:** Eddie's on it! [Laughter] He passed it on to Eddie.

**Faith:** His heart chakra's at 53. Things have gone down.

**Mom:** Okay, it's okay.

**Faith:** It *is* okay. You know he is out there in this crap.

**Mom:** [Reading the comments]

> *Is Trump a Freemason member?*

I wouldn't think so, right? [Takes a drink]

**Faith:** He has connections and affiliations with them but he's not a Freemason member. The Freemasons are all the Illuminati. That line, that lineage, goes back 26,000 years. That's when all this began, you know, the rituals in ancient Egypt and ancient Sumeria.

I actually was guided by my guides for the year, leading up to this, to read all these books into all this sort of information. So, it is an ancient order.

**Mom:** Right. I need a cigarette.

**Faith:** His throat chakra is still at a hundred percent.

**Mom:** Yippee!

[Speaking to the commenters] Robin has been cracking us up since I woke up this morning, which I have no idea what time that was.

**Faith:** 57, the third eye.

**Mom:** Nice.

[Speaking to the commenters] I thought he was gonna come in and give some jokes.

**Faith:** Six percent crown chakra.

**Mom:** Six percent crown chakra!

[Speaking to the commenters] He gives jokes when he wants to give jokes. This is kind of how he is. He loves to tease Father over here.

Thanks, David, for going over to the MeWe chat and letting them know that we have a live meeting that everyone can join. Participate in Heaven on Earth.

31 Love Beings! Yippee! 16 likes! You guys are awesome. Thank you, guys, for liking the video.

That's so wonderful, Joy. You know, my oldest son, he's 23. Well, my son in physical form, he was born on Christmas Day. He was five weeks early. I went into labor with him when I was six months pregnant and I decided to allow the doctor to put me on bed rest so that I could have him in a healthy state. So, he was born five weeks early. He was five pounds. This little boy, little baby on Christmas.

Oh, Thanksgiving! No, Thanksgiving is, like, one of my favorite holidays because my birthday is November 30th. So it was always around that Thanksgiving Day. That's wonderful! Christmas babies, full of presents.

**Faith:** I got a little, like, boop.

**Mom:** Boop! [Laughter]

[Speaking to Faith] I was just telling them about this amazing video I just watched.

**Faith:** Which one?

**Mom:** I sent it to Michael to get posted. It was an hour and a half, but she, um--

**Faith:** Nails it?

**Mom:** Well, her son killed himself in 2016. And now I was contacting her with messages about the New Earth and The Event. And he calls them with the Cosmic Dance. He goes, "It's about to happen, the Cosmic Dance." And he goes, "It's over."

**Faith:** We should try and contact her.

**Mom:** I got you the phone number.

**Faith:** Yay! Is she an American?

**Mom:** Not her, but I got the interview guy.

**Faith:** Okay, amazing.

**Mom:** I forgot to call, so you're going to call him.

**Faith:** We definitely will get on to her.

**Mom:** Yeah, and him as well.

Capricorn! [Points to Faith]

**Faith:** Pretty strong Capricorn in my chart.

**Mom:** 37 Love Beings! Yippee!

**FM:** It's early for that count.

**Mom:** Yeah. It's wonderful, you guys. You guys are catching on. Something's going on.

Robin! "Maybe," he says. [Laughter] There goes him and his jokes.

[Speaking to the commenters] Yes, time is an illusion. The only thing which exists is the Present Moment of Now. There is no past, there is no future, just now. And welcome home!

**Faith:** Oops. Can't see who likes--

**Mom:** What are you doing?

**Faith:** I was just looking to see--

**Mom:** To see what?

**Faith:** To see who was in here.

**Mom:** Oh, okay.

**Faith:** I wonder if Joel from that last session came in.

[Speaking to the commenters] Mother's actually anticipating being introduced to the world before The Event. So, as soon as she goes to the starships and integrates with her light body, then the introduction will happen. And the Event will be a bit after that, as far as we understand.

**Mom:** There are three beings currently in the field who are ready for the starships. So, we have our Trinity Energy ones kind of spinning off, who ate a whole bag of chips. [Laughter]

[Motions to Buddha] He's, like, spread out. I was like, "You ate a whole bag of chips!" It was, like, this big, I think I told you already, but it was funny and he wasn't happy about it.

[Speaking to the commenters] Yes, I will be announced to the planet, to humanity. This is my planet. This is not Trump's planet. This is not your planet. This is not Illusion's planet. It's mine to give to all of you, and that's what's happening.

And this has been in process for the last, well, 19 billion years, but per se, let's just give it 13. [Laughter] Like, this part of the divine plan. If you're not in service, you're not in right action.

**Faith:** Service to love. Mother is love. She's the best example of what love is.

**Mom:** Is any--Okay. Nobody else is having problems? Okay. Reboot your--What does that...?

**Faith:** The modem? Oh, you mean the internet thing?

**Mom:** Yeah.

[Speaking to the commenters] There's Alex! You guys are being consistent. That is going to raise your--I can't wait to see the checks tonight. Oh yeah, because I had two frickin' sucker vampires in here. I mean, I was experimenting, I wanted to see the effects. Obviously, we got to see what happens and we have trolls in the room pulling energy.

**Faith:** Yeah, that's why they do it.

**Mom:** Suckers! Suck, suck! [Lights a cigarette]

[Speaking to the commenters] Yeah. Energy vampires. Exactly, man.

However, you know, like I was sharing, if you come in the field and you have any type of that energy, you're going to get *sick*. You're gonna frickin' wanna run as fast as you can.

Like I said, we've already had it happen. We had Sadie, she was here less than 24 hours and she bailed. They didn't even say anything to anybody, just left.

How disrespectful, but however, you know, that is how the EGO is. It hates me. The white trash programming hates me. It can't stand me. It's been so interesting to experience, to observe, wow.

33 Love Beings in the house! Thank you, loves, for being here. In about 20 minutes, we'll start doing the checks. Do you guys have any questions?

☆★★★★ 73 ★★★★☆

**Mom:** Hi Ariel. Oh, I love that name. So beautiful. Aww. I love you all.

[Reading the comments]

*How to activate the right brain?*

Just what you do is ask, just simply ask, command the angels to help your right brain take over your left brain. That's it. That's how simple it is. [Laughter] Again, I mean, I do daily meditations, two hours at least.

You know, gratitude is where it's at. Be grateful for everything. I cut cords every single day with everything and everyone, and I reattached my energetic cords to everything which is real, which is pure, which is whole, which is true, to miracles, to magical synchronistic events. That is what's real. Attitude of gratitude.

I'm in constant--the back end of me, like, I'm speaking here to you guys. [Points to her face] But this back end of me is like, "Thank you for love everywhere present. [Points to the back of her head] Thank you for miracles. Thank you for the highest states of laughter and joy and happiness. Thank you for abundance. Thank you for all dreams of love coming true." So, this is what's running in the back for me and that's real.

It's very simple. This is not complicated. What I do is every day I say "I cut cords with everyone and everything, and then I reattach all my energetic cords to anything which is whole and real and true and pure."

So, let me get to Brian's question. [Reading the comments]

*Can you explain the synchronicity in more detail? I'm confused on whether it's higher self that plans synchronicity out prior, or if it's angel messages or both.*

Okay. In the Present Moment of Now, we experience synchronistic events and synchronistic events are our guideposts that let us know that we are present in the moment of now. So, the angels are there. It's multi-dimensional.

And synchronistic events have been happening forever. It's just, humanity has been asleep in the illusion and they're missing it because the EGO cannot see synchronistic events or experience it. So, as long as you're present in the moment of now, that's it. It is really that simple. And then you follow your synchronistic events in the present moment. I mean, we get thousands here in the field. The EGO is distracted, you know? So, the soul, who's actually inside, misses--yeah, there it is, 444! That's the angels all around us! [Takes a drink]

[Reading the comments]

*Mother, are you the one source of everything in all existence? And if so, did you create the Father? And who are the beings with the symbol of the V who thought they were the only ones in all of existence?*

Let me get to déjà vu. Déjà vu is because we've already done this before. So, it's like we already did it and we were going backward to actually have the experience. That's the best way I can explain it. So, yes, I am Source. I am the Mother of All Creation.

**Faith:** [Enters the room] Coffee is a-brewin'.

**Mom:** I am also a great-grandmother. Now, I'm still attempting to figure out what all – I mean, they told me this information in 2013, in December, that I was great-grandmother, but I didn't understand what they were talking about.

I mean, I could barely even get that I was Mother God, let alone Mother of Creation, and then great-grandmother. And so, I asked them, "Who created me if I created everything and everyone?" All the angels just look at me. So, I don't have an answer. It's like divine intelligence just came out of nowhere.

**Faith:** As Robin showed it to me, it was like, there were just these forces, like--

**Mom:** These energies. [Lights a cigarette]

**Faith:** These energies. I'm not sure where they came from, but it was the forces of love and the unknowable, the two frequencies that the rest of the universe lives within. Earth is the only one that does not live within true reality, which is the two frequencies. And they, like, kind of collided together and formed consciousness.

**Mom:** Yes.

**Faith:** That's what happened when love and the unknown mix. They formed this consciousness that was Mother. And then from her own essence, she created Father, which is where the allegoric story of Eve creating Adam from her rib comes from.

So, and then it was created. And from there they created the 144,000 and then the rest of creation. But you know, the full kind of reconnection comes when we assimilate back into true reality.

**Mom:** 48 Love Beings in the house! Angel! Yay! No dancing anymore. No EGOs can enter heaven.

**Faith:** Nope. Sorry.

**Mom:** Not even one. [Laughter]

Robin! I asked him if he was gonna chime in tonight. You're welcome.

[Reading the comments]

> *Mom, is it possible to remove everyone's EGO on earth without wiping them out?*

I fucking wish, that is like a dream come true. If I could do that…

**Faith:** Mother has to honor free will.

**Mom:** [Shakes head] Can't.

**Faith:** If Mother could just wave a magic wand – and I did make her a magic wand, can I show them?

**Mom:** Yes.

**Faith:** [Waves a homemade wand in front of the camera] I made this for Mother last night. It's got a bit of selenite in it. Look at my extremely creative capacity. Woo!

**Mom:** [Laughter]

**Faith:** If she could, wouldn't she have done that already? Probably.

**Mom:** Yup. Absolutely.

**Faith:** So, it's free will. She does everything for us.

**Mom:** You guys have no idea, really.

[Speaking to the commenters] Robin's saying in about 13 hours.

**Faith:** She has to honor everyone's free will.

**Mom:** I don't know, Robin's just telling me 13 hours or something. [Laughter]

**Faith:** Thank you, Shelly! [Blows a kiss]

[Speaking to Mom] Did you show them your full dress yesterday? Like did you stand up and give them a full view of the dress?

**Mom:** I don't know. I think so.

**Faith:** Well, the dress that went on yesterday, it was like Belle from *Beauty and the Beast*. She looked like the Fairy Godmother.

And then, I was like, "Oh my God, the Fairy Godmother is Mother's higher self from the lower self." And then I was like, "I need to go make a wand." I went away for a little bit and came back and was like, "A wand!" She was like, "Okay."

**Mom:** [Laughter]

**Faith:** [Speaking to the commenters] Oh, you missed it? Alright. Let's do it again. [Waves the wand in front of the camera]

**Mom:** [Speaking to the commenters] Yeah, I don't know what's happening in 13 hours. I won't allow Robin to tell me, 'cause I really just, I'm done about it. I'm just done. They're like, "We're doing this. We're doing that. We're doing..."

You know, it's all an experiment and it's like I'm a guinea pig and you know what? I'm gonna let it go.

**Faith:** Every day Mother wakes up, she's like, "Okay..." And it's like, you know, I don't know if you spoke about Sadie and the Unified Field?

**Mom:** A little bit.

**Faith:** So, you know, Sadie didn't last 24 hours and she didn't spin out or anything. She was just totally not up for it whatsoever.

**FM:** Distrustful!

**Faith:** Very distrustful. And to Buddha, she was like, very--I mean, Buddha did go downhill...

**Mom:** Oh God.

**Faith:** As he does. He has an amazing, huge capacity for light, but also has a huge capacity of dark. So, he goes there sometimes and we are just like, "Oh, that's alright."

But he was, like, screaming. His eyes were all black and she was just like, "I'm not safe." And she's like, "I'm going to a hotel." We're like, "If you leave, then you are leaving. This is not a joke. This is not just some, like, drop-in."

**Mom:** [Raises her arms] We just hit 40 Love Beings!

**FM:** It's increasing every day!

**Mom:** Sorry for my armpit. I'm, like, doing stuff.

**Faith:** The earth is pain and suffering. Everybody who is here is in pain to one degree or another. The rest of the universe that lives in true reality, unique consciousness, looks on earth, and is just devastated that we continuously are so lost.

**Mom:** [Speaking to the commenters] He loves it! [Lights a cigarette]

**Faith:** Mother was getting thousands, millions, trillions of prayers in the etheric. People just praying for peace, praying for happiness. And it is heartbreaking 'cause they're her children. So, she was like, "You know what? Fuck this noise. This is going to change. We're going to ascend the planet."

And the 144,000, our entire purpose and essence is expansion of light. Everywhere we've gone with Mother, we've expanded the light.

**Mom:** Co-creation.

**Faith:** Yeah. And on earth, the light expansion is non-existent. Everybody just goes deeper and deeper into the programming, the bullshit, the EGO, the unhappiness. Very few people die happy, everybody on their deathbed has regrets and shame, and pain. Fuck that! None of that exists.

So yes, we have to wipe EGO completely. It is more than a plague, more than a disease. It is like--

**FM:** Hell?

**Faith:** Yeah. Earth is hell. Once you get to the understanding of what heaven and true reality is, you just can't even fathom how painful existence is.

**Mom:** And I get to watch you guys. I'm in perfect states of joy. You guys are all...[Makes gibberish noises] Even though I've had to go through several different traumas and healings as a result.

**Faith:** It's never taken your vibration down.

**Mom:** No. Well, I almost did last summer. I was spiraling downward. I'm like, "I left my three children for this?! For humanity to rape me, steal from me, and just take everything from me?" I was depleted, I was done with it, but Robin, he was there.

**Faith:** You unlock that belief for yourself. Fear is *False Evidence Appearing Real*. And every moment you choose fear, your consciousness goes into fear. The way to unlock that is to stop choosing fear, choose love in every moment.

**Mom:** That's right. [Takes a drink]

So, I've had moments where my vibrational frequency spiraled down and last summer was one of them. When I had a being in the field who was a part of the team that left in the middle of the night. And he took every money that I had for the Crystal Schools. $12,000 I had saved for the Crystal Schools. He stole it. I was absolutely devastated. At the same time--

**Faith:** He took your car as well, right?

**Mom:** No. He had his own car. At the same time, the same moment that happened, Facebook kicked us out and wouldn't let us back in.

**Faith:** A hundred thousand members.

**Mom:** No, we had about 50,000.

**Faith:** Was that another one?

**Mom:** Yeah, my Galactic Free Press one. I had over 150,000 on my Galactic Free Press Facebook that got stolen. You guys have no idea. I mean, for me to be still standing here...[Laughter] And we let him keep his balls. Anyone who betrayed me--

**Faith:** Is gettin' it.

**Mom:** Yeah. You don't get to go home into the light if you betray me, let's just say that. I mean, I am full-forgiveness, but their level of betrayal was so deep that there's nothing I can do.

**Faith:** The dark is EGO. Can I explain this, the vibrational scale?

**Mom:** Yeah.

**Faith:** So, it's going to be backwards because of the camera, but I'll just explain it.

[Holds up a chart to the camera] So, this is the vibrational scale of consciousness. I'll have to keep it here. [Points to left-hand-side of chart] This is zero, absolute absence of light, absence of all that is. Evil, right here.

[Points to the right-hand-side of chart] This is a thousand. This is complete enlightenment. This is Mother's vibration always, of course.

And everything from zero to 200 is a life-draining state. Dark. You have dark in you if you have EGO, period. The dark lives within us, nowhere else, not without, only within.

**Mom:** That's correct.

**Faith:** So, everything from zero to 200 is EGO, life-draining vibration. This includes things like shame, guilt, apathy, fear, generally. What else have we got here? Desire, anger, pride, arrogance, superiority – thinking you know better – sound familiar?

**Mom:** [Laughter] Sounds familiar?!

**Faith:** All of these are EGO traits. And so, over 200, up to 1000, is divine traits, life-enhancing traits. Courage, reason, love, joy, peace, happiness, honor, respect, wisdom, trust, truth.

And so, you can be really happy at a state of joy. And then someone comes in, knocks into you, and you get triggered and you lurch down to anger. You're like, "Grrr!" In that moment, you are embodying dark. You've chosen to allow that vibration to take you to anger, which is 150.

So, every being who has not had EGO death is light and dark, divine and sin. And so, we have to transcend out of EGO completely to only be light. And at the moment, there are 16 beings on earth who have had EGO death.

**Mom:** 39 Love Beings in Love's Room!

[Speaking to the commenters] Yeah, love, you're going to be reunited very soon. He's with you, your dad...son. I know, you have to go through the grieving process. You have to go through the seven stages of grief. Please Google that, or you can find it on the website as well.

**Faith:** I've had four different beings in the sessions say that I've been with them in, like, visions and in their dreams and stuff. Faith is with everybody who needs faith. My essence is that of faith.

So, it's funny, Buddha, he went through a portal. When he went into his dark place, he went through a series of portals and it was all these disturbing dark images. And they were like, "Come back, come back." And they're trying to get him back. And he was standing on this threshold. And then I just came in and I was like, "Buddha you've got to come back, come back this way. And have faith in the journey."

And I seem to be appearing to people for that exact reason, for faith. So, it's not so much me as my embodiment but more me as my essence who's there.

[Speaking to the commenters] And Shelly, I do know that when Paul, when he started this journey, he was saying that you were a bit fearful and a bit scared of all the experiences he was having. And it's so beautiful because I felt your essence and what an angel you were.

So, faith is something that will be consistently needed for you because there was that doubt or that fear of it. And so, it's that essence of faith that pulls us through. Everyone has got to have faith.

**Mom:** [Sings] Gotta have faith, faith, faith. George Michael!

40 Love Beings still here!

**Faith:** And I love you so. I imagine I would come and visit you.

**Mom:** Of course! Thank you.

[Reading the comments]

*But who created the dark and who created the black?*

The darkness came from aberrations that came from Jehovah. Jehovah was one of Father and I's sons who decided to branch off from us, from the unity, basically from creation, and decided that he was going to be God without God.

And he began creating all these aberrations and Father and I were like, "Oh shit, I have to go clean this crap up, all this fucking bullshit."

**Faith:** Like black holes and unconsciousness.

**Mom:** Like, what? 43 Love Beings! That's a broken record! [Claps]

**Faith:** 5:00 pm on the dot.

**Mom:** And so, we developed a plan to take care of it. And it's taken us 19 billion years and we're at the end right now. Very end.

**Faith:** All of these aberrations and anomalies were collected up by Father as he went through the dark. You know that scale I just showed you? Father went down to zero. And Mother was at a thousand.

**Mom:** Well, I'm not gonna go there. Robin's like--I'm like, "No!"

**Faith:** [Laughter]

**Mom:** I'm not going there!

**Faith:** Does he keep saying it?

**Mom:** Robin's talking to me about something, I don't want to know. [Laughter] Tell me later.

**Faith:** Yeah, so, those aberrations and anomalies were put in the center of the consciousness scale.

**Mom:** [Speaking to the commenters] You will be able to see him again. Yes, you're just releasing, Sabrina.

[Reading the comments]

> *Mother, is it "We are in such a hurry and ascending earth right now after the removal of the cabal"? Or "Because we must do it as soon as possible"?*

There's no defense against the Cabal, the Cabal are gone. We threw them into the Galactic Central Sun. So, all we're dealing with right now on the planet is EGO.

**Faith:** It's also a full moon today.

**Mom:** I took care of the Reptilians, the frickin' Anunnaki, the freaking Reptoids, dildo--[Laughter] Robin! Stop! That was funny! Okay. Dildo people! [Laughter]

**Faith:** The reason we're doing this so quickly is because Mother is in excruciating pain.

**Mom:** Yes.

**Faith:** A lot of her time she's having to use her tools--

**Mom:** Extreme everything.

**Faith:** You have no idea the extent of her organ damage. This is from processing all of our bullshit, all of the EGO. It just can't be understood.

**Mom:** I know.

**Faith:** Last full moon in Virgo, new moon is in Virgo. Transformation. Getting to the truth of it. The deepest truth is in new moon Virgo.

**Mom:** [Speaking to the commenters] There's David!

**Faith:** David's funny.

**Mom:** He is fricking funny as shit. He always makes me crack up.

[Reading the comments]

*Will the ships ever show themselves to the world?*

"They are!" says Robin.

**Faith:** Once the New Earth is here, everyone's going to live here. The Inner Earth are coming out, all the Pleiadians, Arcturians. This is our home.

**Mom:** Yes, they have bombed me, I've had knives, they tried to kill me 34 times. It's all in the documentation and all on video, by the way.

**Faith:** And I've written lots of posts about it, too.

**Mom:** [Laughter] Oh, you guys. Oh, shoot. I hit my knees again.

**Faith:** It's begun! You guys have got invitations.

**Mom:** [Laughter] Alright. So, let's get to the checks, everybody. If you guys have any more questions before we get to the checks?

**Faith:** And say Yippee if you want a check!

**Mom:** Yippee!

Where's Angel [a dog]? Where's Angel at?

**Faith:** I don't know.

**Mom:** Okay.

**Faith:** Floating about, being a dog.

**Mom:** Being a dog!

[Speaking to Faith] So, Angel, now he's about what? Four months old?

**Faith:** I think so.

**Mom:** So, he's about four months old and he always wants to bite, you know how puppies are that bite bite bite. 'Cause they're teething.

[Speaking to FM] You want to write down the names, Father?

**Faith:** He's on it.

**Mom:** Well, Father's on it. We'll give him a mark on the board.

Robin! [Laughter]

So, Angel puppy, he's going to be big, like we said, he's going to be over a hundred pounds. And he's so sweet. So, he's been doing this biting thing. Now I look at him, I'm like, "Don't bite Mommy!" And he, like, goes into this mode, like, "Okay, no bite Mommy." Then he bites his tail now. So, he's gotten past continuing old biting to once I say that, he's like, immediate bite tail. [Laughter]

[Reading the comments]

*Who was the devil? And I don't mean Satan, the EGO. I mean the devil as a being, as soul.*

There's no such thing as a devil. If you take the word backwards, it spells lived. You're living, experiencing. There's no such thing as a devil.

[Points to her armpit] Look how much...Man, I'm sweating. Must be warm. [Laughter] I'm good like that. Ask these ones, these ones over here.

[Points to FM] Father, how 'bout that? I blow you away all the time?

**FM:** [Nods] I like it.

**Mom:** [Laughter]

**FM:** I love your laugh so much.

**Mom:** "Orange-ya happy?" says Robin. Orange is Robin's favorite color, by the way.

So, just waiting on Faith to come back, she's getting coffee for everybody.

**FM:** Anybody else want to put in a Yippee for checks?

**Mom:** [Reading the comments]

*Mother, can you tell us the story of Jesus?*

What exactly? What exactly would you like to know? Can you give me a specific question?

Yes, I was Jesus. I was told that in 2007 by the angels. And then I got in contact with Aleister Crowley and he told me that I was *not* Jesus, so I let it go. I was like, "Oh, I wasn't Jesus. I don't know, it was supposed to be masculine, right?"

However, in 2014, the information--

[Speaking to the commenters] No, Sananda is not Jesus. Sananda is a starship captain. Christopher Reeves and his wife that was down here-

Yes, I was crucified. I have the whole thing documented. I went back through the timeline. I experienced it all during a mushroom trip that Saint Germain took me on.

Anyways, Yippee! Sananda's a starship captain. Again, like I said, Christopher Reeves and his wife--

No, Sananda was not Patrick Swayze. Patrick Swayze is Sanat Kumara.

[Reading the comments]

*Did it hurt?*

Yes, it did very much. So, I was hung up for 10 days on a board straight, like straight up. And then they turned me upside down for 10 days. And after 20 days, I left my body.

I was looking at everyone. It was so fascinating because I saw all these beings looking at me and I'm like, "They're just watching me die." Like it was no big deal. I could see all this and I started screaming.

I had nine people in the room that were not on mushrooms that were just in the experience with me, watching and documenting. And so, they said I went into, like, whore. I was just in extreme, excruciating pain. I started screaming and, through the experience, then I'm watching all of them look at me die.

And then I hear someone on the right-hand side, like a masculine voice. I'm pretty sure it was Father. [Points to FM] Pretty sure it was him who said, "Look, you guys, you just killed your God." And then I came out of it.

They also had me--they took me through the timeline when I was Joan of Arc. So, I was Joan of Arc. I remembered that whole lifetime in 2001. The angels brought it to me, I didn't even ask for it. I was like, "I'm not asking." They just, like, downloaded the whole thing into me.

And I'm like, "Ah, sh--. I was Joan of Arc?" And then I was like, "Why was I Joan of Arc?" You know, all this stuff. But I grasped that lifetime and I was able to download all the courage, and the strength, and everything that I had during those moments, to bring forward into this lifetime, to bring it back forth so it would help me with the Mission. And I had no idea yet that I was about to embark on a Mission.

**FM:** Are you good, Mom?

**Mom:** [Speaking to Faith and FM] What is going on? What are you doing?

**Faith:** [Off-camera] We're just doing this until it's boiling.

**Mom:** Robin says you're retarded.

**Faith:** I don't--I'm sorry.

**Mom:** You're being retarded. Oh, boy.

[Speaking to the commenters] Yes, Jason. Absolutely.

I don't even know. See, this is how it goes with me. I have no idea. I'm so present, I have no idea what I said one second ago, who knows? [Laughter] I have to depend on the angels and Robin.

Hi Ryan, I love you. I know you're going to be here soon. We have lots of beings who are on their way, and I'm going to go back to Katherine just for a moment.

Now back in 2011, I started realizing that there were beings – what I call handlers – that started appearing in the Lightworker community. And I started calling them out.

Now what handlers are, um, are beings who have been programmed and conditioned by the Cabal – old controllers – to infiltrate the community. And how they did it is they would give you half-truth and then the rest of it was fantasy.

Oh yeah, I was talking about Joan of Arc. When I went back to the timeline, I had to re-experience them frickin' burning me. That was frickin' horrible. Fuck. But not more horrible than the Jesus thingy. [Laughter] Even though, because the Jesus thingy was drawn out, like, 20 days. The fire thing, it was, like, immediate and I was back up and on the starship, but you know, it was still an experience.

[Speaking to the group] What was I just talking about?

**Gabriel:** Joan of Arc?

**Mom:** No, no. I was talking about something--

**Gabriel:** Lightworker infiltration?

**Mom:** Okay.

**FM:** Thank you, Gabriel.

**Mom:** So, I watched the handlers starting to come in and Katherine was one of them. And I was looking at her information and I was like, "Okay, well, there's truth there, but the rest of it's not true."

[Laughter] I've got your number, Robin! He's like, "I got yours!" [Laughter] What number is that? "One!" [Laughter] Thank you, Robin!

So, what I realized through reading the messages from her, what she was doing was using her mind control to peek into the Unified Field to gather information out of my field. And then report on it, claiming-

[Off-camera, an unidentified person belches repeatedly]

**Mom:** [Speaking to the group] Incense, please.

--that she had gone through it and that she was experiencing it. I was laughing my fucking ass off. [Laughter] And I caught her doing it and I called her out. And as you can see, we don't hear anything from Katherine anymore. When's the last time you heard from Katherine?

There's the handlers I caught, I caught them all.

**Faith:** I can get started on the checks.

**Mom:** Yeah. "Just one moment," Robin says.

**Faith:** You've got 40 minutes.

**Mom:** Yeah, it's okay. Alright. So, I'm going to hand the Field right now over to Faith so she can do your checks with you guys. I am the greatest, greatest being that ever existed in all creation. Robin will confirm. [Laughter] Robin!

Anyway, again, we have a lot of beings on the way here. We're so excited. It's unfortunate that Sadie did what she did.

**Faith:** She snuck off! We were like, "Where's Sadie? Oh no!" And then her car was gone and then she was gone.

**Mom:** [Shrugs] She ran.

**Faith:** So, she didn't leave in honor, either.

**Mom:** No.

**Faith:** Total lack of integrity.

**Mom:** Betrayal. She betrayed me. She will be sent to the Galactic Central Sun for recycling.

**Gabriel:** That's what you get!

**Mom:** I love you so much. [Blows a kiss] Alright, you guys enjoy your checks.

# XII

## CONVERSATIONS WITH GODDESS MOTHER GOD (PART 1)

### 37.9964° N, 105.6997° W

*"Try to remember your God down here. She's a trip."*

**AUGUST 11, 2018**

---

**Mom:** "Gaia? Who the fuck is Gaia?" No clue. Call my friend up, I said, "Who's Gaia?" He said, "That's Mother Earth." I looked at the angels and I'm like, "What the fuck are you talking about, angels? I'm not Mother Earth!" [Laughter]

**El Morya:** And you talked to Jesus.

**Father:** She's a little bigger in the hips.

**Group:** [Laughter]

**Mom:** And this continued. Another year goes by, comes back around, "Okay. You're God!" [Laughter] What?!

And then all of a sudden, I told you guys that story...the Square Bob songs...?

**El Morya:** SpongeBob SquarePants?

**Mom:** Huh?

**Pam:** *The Real Slim Shady?*

**Mom:** *The Real Slim Shady.* All of a sudden, as soon as they're talking to me about God, and then it just pops up in my YouTube: "Will the real Slim Shady please stand up?" I'm like, "What?!"

**Group:** [Laughter]

**Mom:** They do a lot of things like that. I feel the biggest, one of my biggest synchronicities is when I came out of that meditation.

So, I was guided to meditation through a rainbow tunnel. And I was going through--my right brain was going into my left brain and came upon the door, the door that nobody can shut once it's opened. Opened up my left brain, right brain just overtakes everything within moments, I think, within seconds.

And when I sat up, I was like, "I'm in heaven. Heaven consciousness." And I said it out loud to the angels and it took me a moment. And then I was like, "I need to check my email." So, I walk up to the computer, and I was getting these whistleblower reports--

[Notices Kellen leaving the room and calls him out] This is a really important story, Kellen, that you're walking out on.

[Speaks to the group] That's a bitch.

**Faith:** [Laughter] Call it out!

**Mom:** I'll finish it.

So, I walk up to the computer. The whistleblower reports had come in and they were coded. So, it was like, "King, swords, something has the report." And I've been getting these for months. So, one had just come in, and I opened it up and it said, "Breaking news" or something like that, "Gaia has just reached zero point, she's in heaven." And I went, "What?! Holy fucking shit!"

I fucking fell to the ground. There was no way anybody, within moments like that, could have known that information unless they were connected to the Unified Field.

But that was one of my biggest confirmations. At that point, I was like, "Okay, alright, I surrender. Come on, angels."

**Speaker:** When did the hose come down, the hose download?

**Mom:** The what?

**Speaker:** The hose came down from the etheric.

**Mom:** What about the hose?

**Speaker:** You said it hooked up to the back of your neck?

**Mom:** In 2014 is when they downloaded me. I was at the Baca, I was sitting on the bed and they were like, "You know, you're the Mother of All Creation." Oh shit! You know that part!

And then the freaking thing came and hooked up in the back of my spine down here. And they downloaded me with Mother of Creation energies.

And then I brought in Father's consciousness in December of that year, December 16th. Yeah. It's all in the documentation.

**Group:** [Laughter]

**Mom:** Okay, Kellen. Thank you.

**Kellen:** Sorry.

**Mom:** Thank you. [Winks] Just keep it in your heart. [Laughter]

**Kellen:** I felt it as I was getting up but I really gotta go to the restroom. Excuse me.

**Mom:** I was just going to take a moment. I understand.

**Father:** It's not personal.

**Mom:** Yeah, try to remember your God down here. She's a trip. [Laughter]

# XIII

## CONVERSATIONS WITH GODDESS
## MOTHER GOD (PART 11)

### 37.9964° N, 105.6997° W

*"It's simple: Surrender. Surrender to the Present
Moment of Now and there you are, higher self, begin integrating."*

**AUGUST 12, 2018**

**LOVE BEINGS:** Mother of All Creation, Father of All Creation, Archangel Michael, Archeia Faith, Pam of Inner Earth, El Morya, Archeia Hope
**SCENE:** Mother rests in bed with Father and shares wisdom and truth nuggets. The First Contact Ground Crew Team surround them on the floor.

---

**Mom:** …and to reach higher states of consciousness, while the levels, it requires dedication, commitment, perseverance, courage. It's not an easy feat, in that sense, I should say. Because humanity has been so programmed and conditioned to be lazy, dumb, ignorant. [Laughter] "Someone else will do it like Mother!"

It's very common, as I was moving through the levels, starting in about 2007, to see. We had no idea – I didn't – about the programming and conditioning. I had seen it at McDonald's and various things, but I didn't quite make the connection that all of humanity was under this spell.

Environmentally program all the takers, instead of the natural organic state of givers. It took me a moment to because I was in a bubble.

That's right, Rick, he used to say, "You'd make me sing all the la-la's in songs." He said I was in la-la land. [Sings] La-la-la love everywhere present. [Laughter]

I uncovered the real truths, that was fun. Not really, I was devastated. After I uncovered the Cabal and what they have been doing to humanity, I cried for three months straight until I got to a moment where I was like, "Okay, I have to forgive now," so I could push the Mission forward.

**Michael:** The conditioning was so deep that we found out that — especially those with the white programming – that the givers are takers, and that *they* were givers. Even though they were blatantly taking, it was not hidden, not subtle. So, their mind created a fuckery where *we* were the takers, and *they* were the givers.

**Mom:** Right, weird.

**Michael:** That was weird shit.

**Mom:** Because it's blatant. You're spending 24 hours a day, seven days a week, in service to humanity? "Yeah, I'm pretty much a taker." [Laughter] That makes no sense whatsoever, dumb. There's no one on this planet that would do that besides me, that's true.

**Faith:** No one did.

**Mom:** And no one did, that's right.

**Michael:** She was the constant example, even with the beings in the house. All the things that I do, she used to do, and then some.

**Mom:** Well, everything you guys are doing, I did by myself.

**Michael:** Yup. She provided housing, warmth, organic food, great weed, organic tobacco. But she was still a taker.

**Faith:** In that perspective.

**Mom:** In their minds, in their EGO minds. But they were entitled.

**Father:** Game of abundance.

**Mom:** They were entitled to everything I had. Some weird mind.

**Michael:** Yeah, it perplexed me because my upbringing is, like, when you were in someone's house, utmost respect. God help you, if you did not represent the family in a way that's honorable, you're gonna get it.

**Mom:** [Laughter] You're gonna get it. But they do that to us, weird.

**Michael:** Yeah, so it's weird. The whole dynamic is just weird.

**Mom:** Pretty much. Yeah, I'm in conversation with Robin about it. [Laughter]

I am glad the energies have calmed down, though, jeez. Yesterday was...yikes. Did anyone do a New Moon Ceremony?

[Phone rings]

**Father:** Robo-caller.

**Mom:** [Laughter]

**El Morya:** I wrote mine, yeah.

**Mom:** Oh, you wrote yours? Wonderful.

**Faith:** Definitely going to get it in before the energies pass through.

**Mom:** Yeah, Lisa out there said there's going to be a cooling period.

**Father:** [Laughter] Her ass.

**Mom:** I'm like, "What? A cooling period?" I don't see that at frickin' all. I see frickin' heating!

**Group:** [Laughter]

**Michael:** That sounds like wishful thinking right there.

**Mom:** I was going, "We got a cooling period, we can relax."

**Michael:** It's going to simmer down.

**Mom:** Noooo! See the frickin' fires? The whole United States is covered in fires. [Laughter] You really think the energies are gonna get cold? [Laughter] Doesn't look like it to me.

Where are we at with Hawaii?

**Hope:** It's stopped for a moment, but they're still having earthquakes.

**Mom:** Okay, I haven't seen anything out there.

**Father:** Yeah, we're gonna get in a bunch of bullshit from that side of the earth.

**Pam:** There was an eruption in Indonesia two hours ago.

**Mom:** Yeah. Energetically, we're coming into the Harmonic Convergence anniversary. Always an intense period of energy. That was one of the first meditations in this era, whatever that means. [Laughter] There's always an energy, like a flip, during the Harmonic Convergence. It's always interesting to experience and observe.

But every day in the Unified Field, we never know. Now it's the super Unified Field, it's expanding; the 30-miles each way expansions. The energies are penetrating, if that makes sense. For me, it looks like oceans of water, but it's just energy, of course. [Sings] Nobody knows it but me... [Laughter] An EGO can't experience it. A being in the soul, or a being in the heart, can have the experiences of this energy.

**Faith:** They're missing it.

**Mom:** Yeah, not my problem. [Laughter]

**Faith:** You showed them where the river was.

**Mom:** Yeah, you can lead a horse to water but you can't make 'em drink.

**Faith:** You have to do the work.

**Mom:** Mmhmm, but it's simple: Surrender. Surrender to the Present Moment of Now and there you are, higher self, begin integrating. Kellen was saying that how I integrated my higher self was through spending 15 minutes a morning getting a channeling, and that's how I did it. He's like, "Are there other ways?" [Laughter]

I was like, "Bring it on angels, thank you. Thank you for helping me integrate my higher self, I love you." And I say bring it on every day, regardless. Bring it on. If there's anything, they do. [Laughter]

Another good technique to say every day is, "I cut cords with everything and everyone, and I re-attach my energetic cords to everything which is whole and pure and real and true, to miracles, to magical synchronistic events."

And like twin flame situations, our connections are unbreakable, so I can cut cords all day long with Father and it doesn't matter. [Laughter]

**Father:** Rainbow bungees. Rainbow grappling hooks.

**Hope:** You ain't going anywhere.

**Mom:** It's one connection we can't cut. And Saint Germain, he was the one that told me that years ago.

**Father:** Mother, I'll share with you because I was sharing with the kids last night that I've been doing a lot of rainbow sword cutting. And if I could share, it's like, I look at it, I'll see my scalp because it's just round, it's representative of the body, and I cut those cords. And I always get this point where I can't go anymore because it's Mom. So, I adjust to cut all of 'em, and that's been an adjustment just in the last day. So grateful.

**Faith:** Thank you, Mama.

# XIV

## FIRST FRACTAL REPAIR

### 29.0300° N, 82.7159° W

*"I'm going to New Earth regardless of your retardation and your dysfunction against me. I am the planet, I am Mother Earth, and you have raped me and done whatever you did for far too long."*

**APRIL 14, 2019**

**LOVE BEINGS:** Mother of All Creation, Father of the Multiverse, El Morya, Archangel Gabriel

**SCENE:** Sitting on a hotel couch and surrounded by the masculine, Mother joins the daily livestream to answer viewer questions and share her wisdom with humanity.

---

**Mom:** [Crying] So done with them taking from me. I gave it my all, that I know. I'm pretty sure.

**FM:** Yes, you did. You did it. You completed the mission.

**Mom:** Yeah. I'm like, "What?!" Crackheads coming after me because they are fucking crackheads. Fucking whores. Coming after your Mother who created you. That's a fucking whore. I have three years of documentation of atoms coming out of my vagina.

I'm pretty sure you're out of my vagina, that was the case. I don't know, I don't know who created you.

**Group:** [Laughter]

**Mom:** I don't know why it's coming outta *my* vagina. I was like, "Pfff. Fucking crackheads." [Laughter]

Atoms, what are you doing? They're like "Yeah, Mom, we're coming back!" To what? To what you did?

"Yeah, we were dysfunctional." I'm like, "Oh, yeah? Well, you're not going to be dysfunctional around me anymore. Recycled!"

**Group:** [Laughter]

**Mom:** I'm going to get a lot of complaints from EGOs.

**El Morya:** Fuck 'em.

**Mom:** [Laughter] I love it. I'm like, "Hey EGOs, who's your Mama? Lilith?"

**Group:** [Laughter]

**Mom:** Go suck on her.

**El Morya:** Have fun.

**Mom:** Don't suck on me. [Laughter] 'Cause I'm real, whores.

**Gabriel:** Get 'em, Mom.

**Mom:** Who's real, who's not? The one who reveals themselves is real, the one who hides is the fake. So, I'm calling it right out. Hey, light-worker, fake-worker community, who's your Mama?

**El Morya:** [Points to Mom]

**Mom:** Check it out. They can't go any further without me. I'll be watching it. They're like, "We're going to leave her out." I'm like, "Good luck. You want to leave me out? What? Why would you leave me out? I'm fucking God, you fucking whores!"

I know I'm God. Germain tells me every day, "You're God, God." I'm like, "Ah, fuck. I forgot." I forget every moment. But luckily, I have Robin and Germain. They're like, "Hey, remember!"

And I got puppets!

**Group:** [Laughter]

**Mom:** Germain's like, "That's a good one." I got my puppets, whores. You don't got puppets.

Ask Germain or Robin if they're going to help you because they won't.

**El Morya:** Good luck.

**Mom:** Unless you are embodying in love and higher self, what the fuck? We got embodied higher love here, that's all we got in First Fractal. And First Fractal, all of them know if they're not embodying full love, St. Germain, he's going to use his whip and fucking kick 'em out.

**Gabriel:** Yeah, true that.

**Mom:** They're all fully aware.

**Group:** [Laughter]

**Mom:** They [commenters] have any questions? [Laughter]

**FM:** Rare opportunity!

**El Morya:** [Speaking to the commenters] You got any questions for Mother God?

**Mom:** I don't know. I'll take it wherever you want to go. I'm all in it.

**El Morya:** [Reading the comments]

*Lots of love to Mother. Emotionally cleansing day.*

**Mom:** He better cleanse! [Laughter] Purity! Purity!

[Looking around for a cat] Where is kitty? Yeah, come over here, bitch. Fucking whore. [Laughter] I love you, kitty. Bravest kitty of all, I'll say that.

**FM:** It's true.

**Gabriel:** Come, kitty.

**Mom:** Kitty knows. Meow! Meow! What you doing? [Picks up a cat]

**El Morya:** No questions, just Sarah. Sarah jumped on.

**Mom:** Sarah's in there? Sarah! [Laughter]

She asked me, "Was it the chicken or the egg that came first?" I said, "Well, egg cracked, chicken came." [Laughter] You gotta get that one.

**El Morya:** How did the egg crack?

**Mom:** Badda boom. Badda Bing. Boop. You guys are dumb out there.

[Cat loudly meows]

**FM:** It sounded like he's like, "Yeah!"

**Mom:** Of course, he's on my side. He's on my side, he's not on EGO's side. We have to be careful because we can ignite things.

**El Morya:** Yeah, the phone is going to die soon.

**Mom:** Yeah, ok.

**El Morya:** Yeah, it's because we're on stream so it's not enough power to get the questions done. It'll all work out, it's probably best for, yeah, anyway.

**FM:** Yeah.

**El Morya:** We want you guys to explode on fire.

**Mom:** Absolutely, I can possibly do that.

**El Morya:** She really could.

**Mom:** I have a lot. [Claps]

**El Morya:** And that's because you're so dense. I almost lit on fire when I met her. And I'll be honest, for a few days, I feel like I'm burning up. She's like, "You are burning through your own consciousness." I just walk around smiling, "Oh, thank God, it's finally gone." And then, you know, anyway. [Coughs] I love you so much.

**Mom:** And then I kick him in the face. [Laughter]

**El Morya:** Mmhmm. It was one time. FM, how many times have you been kicked in the face?

**FM:** I don't know, more than I know.

**El Morya:** Hey, I'm grateful.

**Mom:** Puke face!

**FM:** She's been known to kick me off the bed.

**El Morya:** Yes.

**Mom:** I'll just kick you away from everything. [Laughter] Splatter! Like a bug.

**El Morya:** Hey, if I get kicked by anyone, it best be by my Mama--

**Mom:** Bug splat!

**El Morya:** --because she is going to do it with love, compassion.

**Mom:** Lovebug splat. I don't know where I am going with that one. [Laughter]

**El Morya:** It's all love.

**Mom:** [Laughter] Like I'm involved in some love bug splat. The angels were like, "Yeah, that's really good." I'm like, "Huh, where's the love?" See, they distract me, fucking whores.

It took me, you know, I can do a lot of things. You guys don't even know what is going on. I watch the lightworkers fucking run around in circles. What's going on? They don't even want to acknowledge me.

**El Morya:** No.

**Mom:** And they have it since 2008, everybody. [Claps] Ten years!

**El Morya:** Spinning for ten years straight.

**Mom:** [Names fake lightworkers]

And I have every right. I have everything. But holier-than-thous, or that you knew more than me, and Love Has Won. Every lightworker so-called-site, you guys are dumb.

Gaia Portal, I love you. [Takes a drink]

**FM:** Grateful, Gaia Portal.

**Mom:** That's it. Every site that is not speaking the whole-truth: Done. Talk to Trump. Guess who's my daddy? Not yours, but you can ask him.

And I'm not kidding, let's go. I'm going to New Earth regardless of your retardation and your dysfunction against me. I am the planet, I am Mother Earth, and you have raped me and done whatever you did for far too long.

I was patient watching, boding it, going through it, and finally, I'm like, "Okay, I'm done. Alright, done." Shit! I deserve, and I am the greatest, grandest being in all of creation.

**El Morya:** Yep.

**Mom:** What do you got? Huh? What're you being? Are you being integrity every moment? I am, how 'bout you? Integrity means that you live your life and love everywhere present, just true reality.

If you're not being this, you're gonna be recycled. I don't have moments to embody dysfunction and sickness and disease, which I constantly have been dealing with. And why I dropped, I mean, I was at 150 pounds embodying light.

**El Morya:** Yeah.

**Mom:** And now I'm, like, 100 pounds. Fifty pounds have dropped off my body because of humanity's dysfunction. Because I'm fighting for my life to be here with you, to stick with you, to love you unconditionally, and I'm not loved unconditionally. And there's the problem. So, I'm dying.

**FM:** We love you, Mama. Thank you for all you've done and all you do in every moment.

**Mom:** The First Fractal here is attempting, but it's just hit or miss. You know, whether they're hitting it or missing it, I'm up here, First Fractal of the evolutionary process of something that has never happened before. I'm a guinea pig, I've accepted the role.

I have accepted full responsibility for the role to be the guinea pig for this, and I do it every day. But then, I don't have anyone else saying, "Yeah, we're accepting this, too." I'm like, "Alright." I just keep going, I don't care who's with me or not.

It's been quite a journey for me, for me to still be here talking and communicating. Everybody is quite a miracle because, after everything, nobody could imagine I could be speaking.

**FM:** That's how you know she's God.

**Mom:** I keep going because I love, not because of how I'm treated because I'm treated like fucking shit.

But the love of my heart knows that my atoms are good. I created them in life, in love, and light, and joy and happiness. It's what I created. It's sad.

**Mom:** And, you know, I fight despite fucking trolls, fucking whores. All my life they've been after me, all my fucking life. This is not anything new to me. How about that? I'm sure each of you can endure being trolled for 43 years of your life as you're speaking about love and truth.

Oh, what? What is anyone going to do about that? What? You want to put me in prison for it? Because I'm speaking the fucking truth about love and reality and love everywhere present? Then come and get me. [Takes a drink] I'm sure my starships would have something for that.

**El Morya:** Yes.

**Mom:** Yes, starships. Robin and St. Germain, yeah. But they want to let you guys know that you all fucked up, you have karma coming, and have fun. And St. Germain is coming through fire right now.

If you would like assistance, Robin and St. Germain are there. But if you're going to continue to screw Mother Source, you got no help. All of it has been retracted now, and it will all come back to Source.

**El Morya:** Yay!

**FM:** Woo!

**Mom:** You're all fucked, sorry about that.

# XV

## FIRE IN THE FIRST FRACTAL

### 29.0300° N, 82.7159° W

*"I will walk around here and take my planet back. And the rest of you can kiss my ass. If you want to take down any part of my platforms, go ahead. I got Donald Trump on my butt. He's on my team. Donald Trump, I love you!"*

## MAY 11, 2019

**LOVE BEINGS:** Mother of All Creation, Father of the Multiverse, El Morya, Archangel Gabriel

**SCENE:** Sitting on a hotel couch and surrounded by the masculine, Mother joins the daily livestream to answer viewer questions and share her wisdom with humanity.

---

**Mom:** Hello, everyone! I love you so. Ok, that's all I wanted to say, simple. [Laughter] Nobody knows, but we do.

Fighting every freaking moment for these energetics. Fighting everything I have, and grateful that Robin and St. Germain are here next to me to make sure that I keep going on and keep going forward despite anything else. Yippee!

**Group:** [Cheering]

**Gabriel:** Yeah, Mama.

**FM:** Way to go, Mom.

**Mom:** [Motions to a cat] Kitty gets up on his perch. Of course, you would. Now you are bathing yourself.

**Group:** [Laughter]

**Mom:** You know, I haven't been on camera. The strength that it takes to be here now and completely embodying 5D, and trying to be here, what a challenge.

It's not easy for anybody in the etheric: Galactics, Robin, Germain, Kryon, Kryola.

**Group:** [Laughter]

**Mom:** Easier right now because we're about to go on an adventure. I don't know. Kryon comes in, he's like, "Yeah!" I'm like, "Kryon's here, that means I'm going on an adventure."

Kryon's been coming into my field since 2006. I'm very familiar with Kryola, and humanity is as well. Lee Carroll has been doing an awesome job bringing Kryon through. But of course, the problem has been everyone's been in the flip against me and Kryon. Kryola's like, "And me!" [Laughter] Okay, Kryola, you too.

Everyone's been in the flip against love, and you know it's the moment. Miracles of May, whatever you want to call it. Germain's like, "What?" He's like, "Is that what you just said?" Okay, anyway.

This is what I get: I talk to masters all day long. Yippee! [Laughter]

It's like, "What do you do now?" I'm like, "I don't know."

They're like, "You're a master." I'm like, "Yup, what do I know? I don't know shit." That's a true master, you don't know fucking nothing. I don't know, I'm like, "What? What is that? I don't know." [Laughter] Nobody knows.

Germain is like, "I don't know shit." Robin's like, "I don't know nothing." Alright, don't look at me then, I don't know shit. Who's walking in the unknown? Yippee! [Laughter] And that's what she gets.

[Takes a drink] It's great water there, Florida water, it's special. [Laughter]

**Gabriel:** Plasma water.

**El Morya:** Holy water.

**Mom:** Adventure water. I'm going to go on an adventure without humanity. [Laughter] Get on my starship and go, "See ya!" They'll be like, "What?" I dunno.

**El Morya:** Maybe?

**Mom:** I've done over 3,000 ceremonies on this planet that I can count. Now my feet have completely given up. [Laughter] They're like, "No more. No more ceremony for you, you're done." I'm like, "Fine." [Laughter] I did the best I could to give everything possible, then humanity's like, "Nope, foot stop." And I'm like, "Alright. Well, then I'll figure something else out. Reach around, foot, I don't know."

**Gabriel:** Reach around!

**Mom:** Atoms of energy, who is your Mother? [Laughter] Figure it out, everybody. Everybody move around.

Cat's asleep, he's like, "I'm not going to tell you anything. I'm not going to help you, not going to tell you anything, you guys are screwed"

**FM:** Yet if we come together to heal our Mother, Facebook and YouTube as one, as we're trying to do--

**Mom:** Jesus Christ, is that a fucking concept?

**FM:** The easiest concept, it should be.

**Mom:** Dumb. They're just dumb.

**Gabriel:** Mama flipped the script quick time, quick time. Everyone will give what they love.

**FM:** You guys all know that there's some level of fuckery out there? They try to block us on YouTube, block us on Facebook, yadda-yadda, you guys know all that shit.

**Mom:** Who are they trying to block?

**FM:** Now you see Mama Jesus, Mama God is right here. The real, the true, beauty at its finest, purity, Christ consciousness. The time is now to gather and support and heal her. Because if you don't give a shit, then you don't give a shit about yourself.

**Mom:** Right.

**FM:** If you have nothing to say, if you have nothing to offer--

**Mom:** And divine love mirror, that's all I am, a projector. If you're in divine love, that gets projected back to you. Fear and divine hate, that gets projected back to you. I'm just a projector.

**FM:** She's Mother, you're glue, whatever you say bounces off her and comes back to you.

**Gabriel:** Mmhmm, nice.

**Mom:** Divine love, man. My curse, my love, my everything. I am. Nobody could stop me, everyone tried. We can put it on a list: How many peoples? [Laughter] That would be a fun game. I'm like, "Wow, oh my God, you tried to stop love? How many peoples?"

"Me, me, me, me." I'm like, "Well, put yourself on the list, put yourself on the list. Get it, get it, fucking whores." [Laughter] You know I was gonna get 'em, they knew too, they know. It's like, "What is she going to do? What?" [Laughter]

Atoms that I saw that came out of me, as my beam, beam out of right action right now, whores. [Takes a drink] What are you doing? Whores. [Laughter] And I was like, "Well, that's a good sound." [Takes a drink]

**Gabriel:** [Laughter]

**FM:** See, this is divinity, she's able to laugh about it.

**Gabriel:** Mmhmm.

**FM:** But if you can imagine for a moment: Creating your children, and your own children are denying the love that you're giving them in all moments. How would that make you feel?

**Mom:** It's horrible. It's absolutely horrible.

**FM:** She's in divine joy all the time. She laughs about it because it's funny, in a way. But for those of us who are trying to gather you, and for those of you who are just waking up, the truth is here right in front of you. And if you don't think it's funny, then you know, get some comedy balls.

**Mom:** [Laughter]

**Gabriel:** But support your Mama, okay?

**Mom:** Don't take anything personal, that's the problem. If I do this [Raises her middle finger], or I say, "Fuck off!" Hmm. "God wouldn't say that!" You know what? God would do all that. And if I wasn't God, and you didn't hear me say that, I wouldn't be fucking God. How 'bout them apples?

**Gabriel:** [Laughter] Mama, get 'em.

**Mom:** [Raises her middle finger to the camera]

**FM:** God is cool as fuck.

**Gabriel:** Cool as fuck.

**Mom:** God isn't a fucking whore, right?

**FM:** Right.

**Gabriel:** Pretty sure of that.

**Mom:** That'd be dumb. Dumb. "I'm a fucking whore!" That'd be re-tarded of me. I will walk around here and take my planet back.

**El Morya:** Woo!

**Mom:** And the rest of you can kiss my ass. If you want to take down any part of my platforms, go ahead. I got Donald Trump on my butt. He's on my team. Donald Trump, I love you!

**Gabriel:** Love you, Papa Trump.

**FM:** [Laughter] Love you, DT!

**Mom:** Donald Trump! Yee-haw! [Takes a drink] They're like, "What is she saying? They're white trash, she loves Donald Trump." Yeah, because I'm not white trash. No white trash people love Donald Trump. [Takes a drink]

**FM:** And that's why they're so triggered about it.

**Mom:** Mmhmm.

**FM:** Because he's doing stuff, supporting Mama.

**Gabriel:** Showing your own white trash.

**Mom:** Yup. That's for sure. It's been shown many times, got a lot of information about that.

Robin! We won't even go there. [Laughter] Robin is my ambassador, by the way, just so everybody knows. [Takes a drink] He's my ambassador between the realms of the etheric and here. Yay, Robin! [Laughter]

**Group:** [Cheering]

**Mom:** Germain's like, "I'm in there too." Germain and Robin. Germain, you're in there, too.

**FM:** Pretty active around here, around these parts.

**Mom:** Active? Robin hasn't been active for days.

**El Morya:** He's been quiet.

**Mom:** Until today.

**El Morya:** Yeah, he came in.

**Gabriel:** Mmhmm, this morning.

**Mom:** Germain was holding the fort down.

**El Morya:** He met dragon, I'll bet.

**Mom:** Yes. I was like, "Dragon, no!" I was like, "It's coming." He's like, "No, keep it at bay!" I'm like, "Ahhhh!"

**Gabriel:** Keeping the dragon away from us dumbass masculine.

**El Morya:** Right?! Grateful. Grateful. Thank you, Germain.

**Mom:** Definitely coming at them, because they're dumb, retarded, out of right action. Dragon sees everything and starts coming after them.

And Saint Germain started to realize that energy, when it started to come, was not helpful for me. I was just...it wasn't good, that's for sure. It wasn't helpful.

The dragon wanted to correct every energetic thing that was out of right action, and it was just too much. Overwhelming.

**FM:** Because it's divine intelligence and it's moving like this. [Motions to the sky]

**Gabriel:** And it's going to get your ass into right action.

**FM:** And that's what humanity's bypassing, that's where you all have to understand Mom's physical experience on this planet. That she's in a body like you and I, and she is walking this planet, and she will again.

We have to honor her physical journey. We have to honor the experience that she had on this planet and come together and heal her.

Because the more atoms that are out of right action, the more that are out there in their own self-importance, that's taking energy from her, from her body. This whole body right here is the planet, it's sacred.

**Mom:** Thank you.

**FM:** So, this is the moment to unify and heal her in this realm, because she's the one that connects us to the next realm. You don't go to the next realm or access it without her, that's the truth.

So, here's your Mother. It's right here, she loves you so much.

[Speaking to Mom] We love you so much, okay? Thank you, Mom. We love you so.

**Gabriel:** Thank you, Mom. Thank you, Mother God.

**FM:** Her body's trying to keep up with the dragon energy, the etheric dragon energy, that's why Germain is there.

Because if she were to come out and correct it the way that she wants to, the way it's supposed to be done, her body wouldn't keep up.

But the more that come together in support in the physical, the more that can be a cushion for our energies to start coming in that way, to start coming online fully again, to correct everything, to put it into right action, which is only done with the highest love, that's all she is. Her body will catch up, her body will heal. It'll be a balance.

Right now, she's just moving so fast, she's so divinely intelligent, she's so smart, much smarter than any of us ever know. She runs circles around all of us, all day, every person in humanity, all day, a million times faster than you'd ever could, okay?

**Gabriel:** [Laughter] Straight-up. Damn, Skippy.

**FM:** We are catching up to her, and she's pumping the brakes for us to catch up to her.

So, we heal her, we gather, we get into right action, we bring abundance, we create abundance, we co-create, and we give to each other. And giving and co-creating and abundance just creates a lotus flower of this rebirthing of a New Earth that we literally have to build. And unification with Mom, we cannot build it without her.

So long as she is ignored and put in a corner, it's not going to happen, lightworkers, all of you out there. She needs to be on the most high, seen as the most high, respected as the most high.

She doesn't demand or command you to bow at her feet. She's one with us all. We choose to put her as the most high because she's the one that bridges it for us.

She is the Rainbow Bridge and it's our honor to be in service to her. Thank you for hearing our Mom, thank you for hearing her.

**Gabriel:** Thank you.

**Mom:** [Crying]

**FM:** You alright?

**Mom:** My feet. [Crying] Okay. Just take me outside.

**FM:** Okay. [Carries Mom away]

# XVI

## DIVINE MESSAGE FROM MOTHER GOD

### 37.9964° N, 105.6997° W

*"Most of the time, I just want to be out of my body and not here anymore. It's not fair to me to sit here while everyone is in dysfunction, continues to choose self-importance, and all of this bullshit crap."*

### JUNE 13, 2019

**LOVE BEING:** Mother of All Creation
**SCENE:** Crying, Mother speaks directly into the camera and provides humanity with an update on her well-being.

---

**Mom:** Greetings everyone. I don't know if this video will go out or not, but angels guided me, of course, to put it out in these moments, these crucial and critical moments. [Crying]

The amount of pain I'm experiencing is beyond human. Like, you can't go there because if you did, you couldn't make it, like, in the comprehension or compassion of it. It's too, too much. I'm doing the best I can with what I have.

I'm working with the Galactics every moment. Robin's here, 'course he's concerned because I've reached over 800 levels of pain. [Crying] You can't comprehend that in human terms.

And I apologize for breaking down but you guys need to understand the situation because, you know, Robin told me years ago that humanity didn't choose me. And I knew what I was facing energetically and we're getting to see the results of that on my physical body. It's disheartening. I'm lucky if I can eat.

Most of the time, I just want to be out of my body and not here anymore. It's not fair to me to sit here while everyone is in dysfunction, continues to choose self-importance, and all of this bullshit crap. Jesus! I've done more work than to have that experience.

Anyway, I did want to share with you guys an update about where I was at. [Laughter] I love you unconditionally. [Blows a kiss to the camera]

Despite anything for me, Love Has Won. [Crying] And despite anyone who has stolen from me, challenged me, raped me, pillaged me, taken me down, called me down, put me in the corner, whatever you had to do – EGO – you're fucking over now. This is my planet. Fuck you, motherfucker. Taker. You don't get to take from me anymore. All givers inherit Planet Earth=Heart. Love you.

# XVII

## YOU ARE THE GREATEST – LOVE HAS WON

### 37.9964° N, 105.6997° W

*"Come on, let's go! Be brave, you fucking motherfuckers.
You came out perfect out my fucking pussy!"*

**JULY 4, 2019**

**LOVE BEINGS:** Mother of All Creation, El Morya, Archeia Faith, Archangel Gabriel, Pam of Inner Earth
**SCENE:** Livestreaming from her bed, Mother hosts a Galactic Dance Party and is joined by members of the First Contact Ground Crew Team. Mother manages the microphone and shares songs and stories with humanity.

---

**Mom:** Going live, well, this is my live. They don't even know what's going on, just perfect, because I don't actually want you to know what's going on.

**El Morya:** [Laughter]

**Mom:** You're so fucking retarded and dumb.

Okay, dragon. Dragon coming in there. Watch out, everybody. Holy shit, I'll fucking come after your fucking EGO, fucking whores. I'm fucking done with you, stupid retardation. Functional reality is coming.

What just happened on earth? And you can fucking fuck off, get it?

I don't know. I'll just--I'll go after them. Looks like three people [watching the livestream]. I'm going to sing a song, maybe you'll get it, maybe you won't. Maybe you're whores, maybe you're not. [Laughter] Maybe you're aberrations, maybe you're not.

**El Morya:** Probably.

**Mom:** And you know what? Fuck off! If you are not supporting love everywhere present, you're a fucking whore. Strike the fuck up and everybody in creation is calling you out, fucking whores!

**Faith:** Oh, we're down to two [on stream]. Awesome.

**Pam:** [Laughter] Trigger!

**El Morya:** Guess they're being too whorey!

**Mom:** [Laughing and mocking humanity] "I am too whorey!"

Fucking whores. You have no idea what the fuck you've been doing.

[Speaking to the group] Is this [microphone to a karaoke machine] on?

**Faith:** It's on. You gotta speak up.

**Mom:** I don't hear anything.

**Faith:** It's an angle thingy.

**Mom:** Alright. Are we fixing my other one? Because it needs a direction as well.

**Faith:** The other microphone, that one definitely works. It's a different brand to the actual machine.

**Mom:** Okay. What's wrong with it?

**Faith:** It's a different brand as far as I know.

**Mom:** Okay. What's wrong?

**El Morya:** We need another battery.

**Mom:** That's what I asked for. Okay, then fucking get the battery, what the fuck? Oh my God.

**El Morya:** I'm going to go serve love and do it.

**Mom:** All of creation is here and everyone is like, "Okay, it's spinning." We are spinning. All of creation is here watching everything going on. It's like fucking crazy, I don't know. I'm live.

[Pans camera across items on her bed] Oh look, there's a pipe. Next to Jasper, bacon flavor treats for doggy, Bugles, unicorn fruit snacks, two pounds of rocks to decorate. I'm grateful. I'm not sure how much I'll get to that, but it's a great idea for the Crystal Children. I'm providing everything like this.

You wanna hear love grabbing his balls? Go. Love's grabbing his balls and it's about fucking time, you fucking whores. Because that's our freedom, not fucking supporting 3D, like…[Makes gibberish noises]. Fuck off, 3D crap. Focus on 5D. That's the reality, that's the truth. The rest doesn't matter, it's ridiculous, it's Whoreland.

**Faith:** [Laughter] Whore-Ville.

**Mom:** Who lives in Whoreland but whores? I don't. Except I'm not a whore and I respect love. What do you guys got out there? Are you respecting love?

Every moment serving love is the answer and the solution to what is happening on this planet. And if you're not a part of it, a part of this solution, then get the fuck off!

Mother Earth says, "I fucking hate you, get the fuck off me, because I only support love everywhere present, period." And everyone supports love everywhere present and the miracles that love provides. I fucking gave it to them.

The good thing about God is that God is not stupid like humanity. Calling your fucking asses out, fucking dumb ass whores, ants. Walking around like you control God.

[Mocking humanity] "Yeah, God! I pray to God."

That's good, I'm grateful that you pray to God. But what did you do in right action for God? "I just laid down like a dumbass whore." Good. That's serving God, serving love, serving yourself? That's whorish, dumbass whorish behavior.

[Laughter] They're like, "Who is she talking to?" I'm talking to you. That's why I keep bringing them up. Hey, whores, I know you're listening. [Laughter]

**Group:** [Laughter]

**Mom:** They're like, "Is she talking to me?" Absolutely. If you're a whore, I'm fucking talking to you, fucking bitch.

**Faith:** [Laughter] It's "Trigger Transformation Hour" for everyone watching.

**Mom:** Transform into love everywhere present and then you're a warrior. All you fucking bitches, then you're a warrior for life. Until then, you're a fucking whore!

**Group:** [Laughter]

**Mom:** I know Gabriel's on the floor. [Laughter] Whore! Whore!

**Gabriel:** [Laughter] Get 'em, Mom.

**Mom:** What do you got, you fucking whore?

**Gabriel:** Love everywhere present.

**Mom:** Right, yes, right. Show it to humanity, then they got it.

**Gabriel:** Would I show it to humanity?

**Mom:** That's your problem that you haven't accomplished.

**Gabriel:** Okay, well, let's get it on then.

**Mom:** Alright. And I have the microphone.

**Gabriel:** Yup.

**Mom:** It's called my microphone.

**Gabriel:** [Laughter] Yes, I love you, Mom.

**Faith:** [Laughter] Rocking in.

**Mom:** What? Wanna rock with me?

**Gabriel:** Yeah, always.

**Mom:** Fucking whore. You can't fucking ride off my fucking coattails.

**Faith:** [Laughter]

**Mom:** Pfff. Fucking get your own fucking coattails.

**Gabriel:** [Laughter] I love you. Shit. Get 'em, Mom.

**Mom:** This is my microphone. I told them I was gonna yell, but when I bought this house, I was like, "I thought this was my house." Come on, police, CPS [Child Protective Services]. Fucking crackheads over there, whatever. Pfff. Come right here. I've been here, fucking whores! I watch you! [Laughter]

And you were gonna kill me! Tell the people! They're like, "Yup. We were gonna kill Mother God."

**Faith:** Yup. Mmhmm.

**Gabriel:** Shit.

**Mom:** They can't deny what they did.

**Gabriel:** No, they can't.

**Faith:** Tried earlier this week.

**Mom:** Done. They're like, "Yeah, she stole from us!"

**Gabriel:** Oh, Jesus, that bitch. Lilith bitch.

**Mom:** Please, everyone, share with everyone the examples of how I stole from you, please.

**Pam:** [Laughter]

**Mom:** No one had anything, nothing! I was like, "Good job you fucking whores!"

**Gabriel:** It never gets old. [Laughter] It never gets old. I love it so much.

**Mom:** I keep going. I was like, "Fucking whores!" They were, like, telling all these lies about me. I was like, "Hey, nay-nay!"

**Group:** [Laughter]

**Mom:** Nay-nays! These whores are lame. And they try to steal everything from me and I was like, "Fuck you." I left for Oregon. I was like, "I'll be back, probably."

I just stole over, I took all my energy. I was like, "I'm taking it with me. You guys are on your own, here in Crestonian land."

**Gabriel:** Yeah.

**Mom:** I was doing my best to bring them up to the portal and they were just fighting me. I was like, "Fuck off, then. Fuck off you fucking whores!"

**Faith:** Woo! Get 'em, Mom!

**Group:** [Applause]

**Mom:** I'll open the portal anyway, you fucking retards.

[Singing] "This is my land, and it's my land, fuck you all, fuck you all..." Here's my foot, football-land, fucking whores!

**Gabriel:** [Laughter] Get 'em.

**Mom:** My land!

**Faith:** Mama's body!

**Mom:** And so, it was so fascinating with Andrew and the Mystic Rose. I was like, "I'm going to kick Mystic Rose." [Laughter] And he's just like, "Bye, Mystic Rose." And I kept telling 'em, like, "I wonder why?"

**Gabriel:** I wonder why? Hmm...

**Mom:** This is me, the rose, coming into Crestone, taking the fuck over. Fucking, fucking whores. They're all scared. They knew. They're like, "Please leave." I'm like, "Huh. Why are you guys scared?"

**Gabriel:** Dunno.

**Mom:** That's interesting, like, "Oh, 'cause you're lying? That's why you're fucking scared?" Huh. Who comes in? Uh oh, the Angels are like, "Oh, shit." Who comes in with the truth?

**Gabriel:** Mama G.

**Mom:** Crestone, Colorado is fucking shaking in their fucking boots-

**Faith:** Woo! [Applause]

**Mom:** --because they fucking know that I have fucking returned and this is my planet. And they can come in or come out. Come in, come out.

They want to take control. They're like, pfff. Come take control, you fucking whores.

They have nothing. Like, "Nope, we don't." Alright. You support me or you don't. I came back to Crestone to take back my planet, fucking whores. They're not takers, they're not. These fucking whores that walk around and think they're in pristine condition of something and they own something? No, I own it, it's mine.

Hannah? Toast. Who else is in here? She's the big one. I'll take everything. I already knew that I was getting everything from that. I didn't know how, when, where, why, what, but I could see it. And Hannah owned most of the spiritual community around here, like every place I tried to acquire, she was trying to block me. I was like, "Pfff. Fuck. I could build gardens here, I can build majestic things. Why are you guys fucking blocking me?" I was baffled.

It's like they knew I could produce it, manifestation. I could build this place into greatness. Abundance for everybody. I was just in a fighting match here. My own energies fighting me. Like, "No! You cannot come here!" I'm like, "Yes, I can! Get the fuck out of my way, you fucking whores!"

**Gabriel:** Yup, get the fuck out.

**Mom:** If you are not in alignment with love everywhere present, get the fuck out!

**Faith:** Woo!

**Gabriel:** Love Has Won!

**Group:** [Chants] Love Has Won!

**Mom:** This is why I needed my microphone, to talk to them because they can't fucking hear me. No matter what action, no matter what website platform I came to Crestone with, they're like, "Fuck you." I'm like, "Guess what? Fuck you."

**Gabriel:** Yup, yup.

**Mom:** You fucking mother fucking whores! Guess who fucking won? When they kept driving me out like I was fucking nothing. Nobody knows what that feels like.

**Gabriel:** Yup, you get 'em, Mama. Fuck 'em.

**Mom:** Prince [a cat] is up, meow! [Laughter]

[Speaking to a cat] Hey, we don't want to hear from you, fucking whore.

**Pam:** Probably hasn't eaten dinner yet.

**Mom:** [Speaking to cat] Yeah, you're just waiting for your fucking dinner. [Laughter] Yeah, we're not here to fucking serve you, you fucking whore.

**Group:** [Laughter]

**Faith:** He's running away.

**Mom:** I know. Pfff. Prince! [Laughter]

**Pam:** Is it ok, I could wait--

**Mom:** I know. "You're live?" Yes, I'm very aware, thank you. Everybody's like, "I don't know what's going on." Like, I really don't know either, but we are live. [Laughter] He's going somewhere.

[Describing her phone] It looks like a blank screen, but yes.

**Pam:** I feel it's been spinning out.

**Mom:** Yeah, it's like spinning. I don't even know.

**Pam:** There you go.

**Mom:** The chat's been going on though.

**Pam:** Okay, there you go.

**Mom:** People are talking.

**Gabriel:** That's good!

**Mom:** I'm like, "Okay." [Laughter] I know I was about to, like, the angels just brought me to them, they want me to sing *Selene*.

**Faith:** Oh, nice.

**Gabriel:** Celine Dion?

**Mom:** Imagine Dragons.

**Pam:** Imagine Dragons, okay.

**Mom:** I went on top of the mountain of Mount Shasta, and I was just like, I was drunk, high, I was just sitting there. I'm like, "Imagine Dragons!" I started blasting it across the mountain as much as I could.

**Gabriel:** [Laughter]

**Mom:** People were stopping by my car, like, "What are you doing?" I'm like, "I don't know, I'm playing music. You enjoying it?" I had no cops come to me whatsoever. I just blasted it, the music, on top of the mountain. It was just, like, bouncing off and people were stopping by the car, like, "What are you doing?"

I'm like, "I have no fucking idea what I'm doing. I'm listening to Imagine Dragons and working it. Let's do it. You know, let's change the whole planet, let's change the whole paradigm, let's do it." You know, and how many moments I brought--Hey!

**El Morya:** Bring it on, Mama! I'm here.

**Gabriel:** Want some more medicine? Want some more?

**Mom:** In a minute. They said I was on livestream, I don't think so unless they can hear me on them.

[The group sets up speakers and music]

**Faith:** Yeah, you're on live.

**Mom:** Alright. Well, let's continue then, what's my next song?

**Faith:** *Selene!*

**Gabriel:** [Speaking to El Morya] There's another one of those body butters there.

**Mom:** *Selene!* That's my song anyway.

**El Morya:** [Speaking to Gabriel] Can you pass me that coconut one?

**Mom:** Hey!

**Faith:** All the love.

**Mom:** Okay.

**Pam:** I'm trying to get the speaker on.

**Mom:** Oh, okay.

**Pam:** Here we go.

**Mom:** Alright, everything. *Selene,* it's my song, that's my song. Woo!

**Group:** [Cheering] Yippee!

    [Song plays & the group sings along]

    Song: Imagine Dragons – Selene

**Faith:** That's YouTube, you got Pandora, Pam?

**Pam:** Oh, no.

**Faith:** Okay. So, that's YouTube search.

**Mom:** Alright, that's fine.

I don't know. It's not me, they're fucking bypassing.

**Faith:** Mom on Skype, Yippee!

**Mom:** Hello?! This fucking...

**Group:** [Song plays & the group sings along]

Song: Nahko And Medicine For The People – Love Letters
To God

**Mom:** Come on, let's go! Be brave, you fucking motherfuckers. You came out perfect out my fucking pussy! Then what do you do? Watch out, fucking Crestone fucking whores!

**Group:** Woo!

**Mom:** You contemplate. I'm going to change every fucking thing of your fucking...Pfff. Crackheads. Cockroaches.

**Gabriel:** Get 'em.

**Mom:** They want to fight me, okay? Ready? Fucking whores! Reptilians. I take over my planet any way I can. And you fucking whores can stay in the fucking background. Cockroaches. Fucking whores. Fucking everything I can to take back my fucking planet. Fuck you!

**Group:** Woo-hoo! [Applause]

**Mom:** Everyone is fucked on this planet without me.

**Gabriel:** True that! Facts.

**El Morya:** Fact.

**Mom:** Sitting here with my fucking broken feet. I've been in constant motion since I was born. Sitting here, it's the most challenging thing.

I'm an Olympic star. You want me to, like, do things Olympic, I can do it and I will. I'm capable of that.

**Gabriel:** It's true.

**Mom:** And then I'm sitting here with my feet like a fucking invalid, with feet that don't fucking work.

I'm the best dancer on this planet. I'm the best of everything on this planet.

**El Morya:** True!

**Mom:** If Simon Cowell were to judge me, he would say, "You're absolutely the most brilliant." I'm like, "Of course." [Laughter] I am!

**Gabriel:** God's got talent!

**El Morya:** [Laughter] God's got talent! You made talent!

**Mom:** Of course I am. I fucking created talent. And Robin's like, "Yeah, you created comedy." I'm like, "Shut the fuck up, you fucking whore."

**El Morya:** There it is. [Laughter]

**Mom:** He's like, "You remember, Mom, when you created comedy?" I'm like, "No, because I really don't like it right now. You can fucking suck your dick and whatever, I don't like it." [Laughter]

Robin's like, "Oh, is that what you want?" I'm like, "Yeah. I don't like these whores, I hate them."

These fucking peoples and these ants and these retardations and dysfunctions and Laurens. The Laurens I have to fucking deal with. It's like as soon as she did all that shit, I was like, "I'm done."

**El Morya:** Fucking whore.

**Gabriel:** Done. You're fucked.

**Mom:** I'm like, "I'm done. I tried to help you, you tried to nail me to the cross, again." Like I was the one that did something.

**El Morya:** Nail in the coffin.

**Gabriel:** Lilith bitch.

**Mom:** I was like, "You're a fucking--you didn't fucking talk to me for three days, bitches coming after me."

**El Morya:** See it a mile away.

**Mom:** You're my snake whore anyway.

**El Morya:** I love you so much.

**Mom:** I know you do. You're my snake whore.

**Gabriel:** Snake whore! [Laughter]

**Mom:** He knows when the snakes are coming.

**El Morya:** Yup, yup. Mmhmm. That's why I'm here.

**Mom:** [Laughter] "That's why I'm here!"

**Gabriel:** You chop the heads off before they come.

**Mom:** He just called himself out. He just calls them out and then I know what's going on. And that's just the way it works with these whores. You know what we're doing.

**El Morya:** You got to take it on and then learn it, and then transform it, and then go, "Okay, well now that's what I learned."

**Gabriel:** ...with Lauren.

**Mom:** She's a fucking whore.

**Gabriel:** And Mom was so nice to her.

**El Morya:** Of course.

**Gabriel:** Shit.

**Mom:** That's how it works.

**Gabriel:** And what she could do is talk about herself.

**Mom:** But you guys got to see the example.

**El Morya:** Yeah, I'm grateful for that. I'm always grateful for that. I see it every time.

**Gabriel:** Yeah. Thank you, Mom.

**Mom:** And that's what I do it for.

**Gabriel:** Yup.

**El Morya:** You take it all on. It's just, you're amazing. Now I try to get everyone to see, I'm like, "Do you see what she's doing?" So we can learn and grow.

**Gabriel:** Shields up.

**El Morya:** Relax, watch, learn, get 'em.

**Mom:** Exactly. It's not a competition. It's just love everywhere present.

**El Morya:** [Laughter] People pull their dicks out and they're like, "Hey! Look at this, hey!"

**Mom:** You have a dick? I didn't even know you guys have dicks.

**Gabriel:** [Laughter]

**Mom:** You have a dick? No, it's not possible, it's not functional in reality. Pfff. Pretty sure.

And this time I'm like, "What'd you say? You're going to fix the dicks?" Yes, dicks don't exist in heaven, I'm just saying. I don't know, I just keep drinking alcohol. Of course, all dicks are judged by that.

Robin! Robin came to me, I was like, "What the fuck are you talking about?" He's like, "Yeah, dicks are all..."

What? Oh shit, fuck. Robin Williams, I'm going to put this in your fucking name, you fucking whore. Are you fucking coming? You want to give your perspective? He's like, "Not right now." I wonder why, Robin? He's like, "Uh, you got a lot of power." Huh, really? Which part, fucking Robin Williams? Do you want me to blast you off right now? 'Cause I will.

Holy shit, Germain! Robin's like, "She's coming after me!"

**El Morya:** [Laughter] Oh, shit! Oh, man!

**Gabriel:** Holy shit!

**El Morya:** You got Germain now!

**Gabriel:** He's like, "I need backup!"

**Mom:** Robin's like, "I need Germain! Oh my God, I need help."

I'm like, "You know what, Robin? Who's going to help you?" He's like, "Well, I thought you were." I am, Robin, but who's going to help the who-who-who?

He's like, "Did you just confuse them?" I'm like, "Absolutely. I'm the fucking who-who-who."

**Gabriel:** I love that.

**Mom:** If I get who-who, I am the who-who-who.

From the time I was, like, two years old, I knew what the fuck was going on.

**Gabriel:** Yup.

**Mom:** No one could challenge me or change me or tell me. I was like, "I got this." Everyone was coming in, like, "Yeah, we can change your DNA and change your thoughts."

I was like, "I don't know what you're talking about. You got fucking nothing and I don't hear you."

My parents are like, "Um, are you trying to talk to 3D people?" I'm like, "No, I don't like them. Crap heads, I don't serve them." My parents are like, "Okay, what do you serve?" I'm like, "I serve humanity in love everywhere present, that's what I serve."

So, if you guys don't fucking get with it, pfff. Fuck off.

**Gabriel:** Get with God-programming.

**El Morya:** Yeah.

**Mom:** I told my whole family, I got 'em with the whole everything and said that's who I serve. And they didn't get a whiff of it or get along. I was like, "You're done." There's no one that wants to serve dumb on this planet.

**Gabriel:** Yeah.

**Mom:** Nobody in creation is like, "Yeah, dumb is prevalent." All over this planet, they're so fucking retarded and dumb that they can't even hear Mother Earth talking. Which is my forte, Mother Earth talking.

**Gabriel:** [Laughter] "Mother Earth talking."

**Mom:** You're not hearing? Hmm. We're going to have a problem, a serious problem. If you fucking back down from me, I'll fucking kill you with my hands.

**Gabriel:** [Laughter] Get 'em, Mom.

**Mom:** Mother Earth! Mother Earth!

**Group:** Woo!

**Mom:** I will kill you with my own hands if you want to fucking kill me. You fucking motherfuckers!

**Gabriel:** [Laughter] Get 'em, Mama! Get 'em!

**El Morya:** Fucking warrior!

**Gabriel:** Yup, baddest warrior of all.

**Mom:** I got this, you fucking motherfuckers! They're like, "Don't talk to me in that way." I will talk to you in any fucking way I respond to because you're my fucking atoms. You came out of my fucking pussy and my vagina. So, welcome home into the light, or welcome home into the darkness, pick your poison.

**El Morya:** [Laughter]

**Mom:** I don't know, I'm just following along with the script that Robin's like--

**El Morya:** [Serves Mother] Okay, princess, here you go.

**Mom:** "Your princess?" says Robin. Like, yes. [Laughter] Robin?

"Yes, confirmed she is a princess, a wild creation. I've been with her for 5 years, I will confirm. She's traveling around, I was hanging with her like a prince." [Laughter] Robin, what a dick. Shit.

**El Morya:** That's fucking awesome. [Laughter]

**Mom:** Oh my God. "I was traveling around with princess. She went to Disney World. I tried to help her."

**El Morya:** We did our best. Fuck.

**Gabriel:** Jesus.

**Mom:** But that was where Robin was like, "Fuck!" He fucking came in, he's like, "I'm ambassador now, fucking motherfuckers. You fucking want to take from your Divine Mother? Fuck you!"

**Gabriel:** [Laughter]

**Mom:** Robin Williams stepped in, he was like, "Fuck you, fucking motherfucking whores. Why are you stealing from your Mother?" His energetics came in.

**El Morya:** Mmhmm. Can't stop it.

**Mom:** I was like, "Alright, I salute Robin Williams."

**Gabriel:** Thank you, Robin Williams! Love you, Robin!

**El Morya:** Thank you, Robin!

**Mom:** Robin came in, he's like, "The fuck are you doing to your Mother?" He was horrified. He tried to understand what was happening. I tried to explain to him what energetics--it was okay, that humanity was doing what they were doing, and he wasn't for it. He was like, "Fuck!"

And then, you know, Robin Williams went into his genius form for me, for us, and he's like, "I'm a genius, I'll figure this out. We have a solution. Look, I know you're hanging in the wind, but we have a solution."

And I told Robin, I was like, "Okay, I trust you, Robin, that we do have a solution for this, that they can stop this on me."

And you have to understand Robin. For him, I'm the love of his life, every moment. So, that's all he's focused on.

**Gabriel:** Thank you, love.

**Mom:** In truth, in reality, all Robin is asking for everybody on the team is my stability, my comfortability, my joy, happiness, because he's all part of it and you guys are too.

**Gabriel:** Thank you, Mom.

**El Morya:** We love you.

**Gabriel:** We love you, Mom.

**Pam:** Love you.

**Mom:** And of course, they tried to steal everything. Robin said, "Fuck off, you can't steal that." Father did the same thing, they did the same thing. All this energy right now that I'm talking about, they tried to steal because they knew.

It's flattering in some senses. Like, okay, thanks for trusting me enough to know that I would do the right thing, and create the right things, and manifest the right things that are in right action, which is the whole thing. This whole fucking planet's deprived. Deprived of the truth, of right action, and that's why I'm like, "Ugghhh!"

**El Morya:** It's not right.

**Mom:** I just have to keep--I mean, these are *my* microphones. I didn't ask humanity for them. I didn't say, "Humanity, provide me a microphone so I can fucking kick your ass!"

**Group:** [Laughter]

**Mom:** And I never said that. I did, though. I was like, "I'm going to fucking kick your ass. How about them apples? You're dumb, you're stupid, you don't know what the fuck you're saying."

I told my whole family the same thing, and they backed down because I know the fucking truth because I am God. Back down!

**Gabriel:** Yup! Get 'em for Mama.

**Mom:** Whores! Whores! [Microphone cuts out] Nope, they fucking cut me off.

**Gabriel:** Batteries?

**El Morya:** Might be.

**Mom:** [Microphone comes back] Whores, back down. Back down you fucking whores.

**Gabriel:** Yup, back the fuck down.

**Mom:** I have--

[Microphone cuts out] No, they shut me off.

I'm going to watch this shit. Here we go.

[Microphone comes back] I am warning you fucking whores: this is my planet, not you motherfuckers'. Pfff. Bugs, they're coming.

**Gabriel:** Shields up.

**Mom:** I don't know what they're doing. Hey! Whores! You want to fucking challenge me, you fucking whores? Let's go, I'm so fucking ready.

**El Morya:** She's got her tools ready.

**Gabriel:** You wanna dance with God?

**Mom:** I gotta dance. Let's dance, fucking whores. We're out here like, "Yeah, you're in Crestone, what you got here in Crestone?"

**Gabriel:** What you got, Crestone?

**Mom:** They're fucking whores. Dumb. Hey! Hey, whores!

They didn't answer.

**Group:** [Laughter]

**El Morya:** A little smack in right action.

**Mom:** Whores! I gotcha, dummies. You didn't think I was coming? Nope. I'm like, "Pfff. It's called 'You're dumb.'" They're like, "No, we didn't think you were coming back."

I'm like, "I didn't want to fucking come back to this fucking whore-hell place called Crestone, Colorado."

**El Morya:** No, she didn't! [Laughter]

**Mom:** I'm like, "Nope." And in fact, I have a radio station on my behalf. It says Crestone's a piece of shit.

**El Morya:** Woo! Stinky!

**Mom:** And it's going to be shouted. Oh, there we go, it's going to be shouted across the planet, you fucking dumb whores. Pfff. Mother of Creation's in your face! Oh, here they go. I'm going to get them, whores.

Actually, don't look at my land because of the whores. Angels were laughing. I was like, "Definitely. I'll take it on." I was looking for it, though. I was like, "I don't even know what I mean." I was just like, "Sure." [Laughter]

I was like, "Where is the whore anyway? I don't know, I'll take it on, though." I thought that's good land, maybe I'll go to Whoreland. [Laughter] Everyone's like, "No!" I'm like, "Why? Is there something I don't know?" I was like, "Just fucking transform it."

It's a Whoreland, you just fucking transform energy, and I don't understand what's going on. [Singing] "This is my land, this is your land…" Where's my land? Maybe I will bring you into my land but I got fucking proprietors.

**Gabriel:** [Laughter] Proprietors!

**Mom:** He's like, "What are you supposed to say in my--"

I don't even know what you're talking about, what is that? Proprietors? What is he saying? Proprietors?

[Technical issue with livestream]

**Pam:** …Almost like you have to shield the transmitter.

**Mom:** Oh shit, oh fuck, the fuck is he talking about? I'm gonna--

**Pam:** Shield the transmitter.

**Mom:** My stomach is starting to roll.

**Pam:** Shield the transmitter.

**Mom:** Oh fuck, it's a transmitter.

Germain, what is Robin talking about? He's like, "You're the main controller of all."

Alright, one moment. I totally--I don't know. No, okay, yes! Alright, got back.

**Gabriel:** There you go, yes! Back up and running [the livestream].

**Mom:** I got to talk to Robin about this shit, I only understand what he's talking about. He's my fucking--

I don't know what the fuck's going on half the time. I'm like, "Robin?" He's like, "Oh, just drink your drink." I'm like, "Okay, thanks."

**Group:** [Laughter]

**El Morya:** Mmmm, tasty!

**Mom:** I'll just drink it.

I'm like, "What do you got, Robin? What do you have to tell me?" It's called, "Don't tell me" and will you?

I could go without it because I know the solution. But Robin Williams and I are right here in the background for humanity like, "You fucking whores! Why are you so fucking retarded and stupid? You have divine intelligence right in front of your eyes." They're like, "Oh, we're dumb." Me and Robin are like, "Yeah, you're dumb."

**Gabriel:** Retarded.

**Mom:** You have Robin Williams and Mother of All Creation in front of your face and they just fucking freak it off like fucking nothing. And me and Robin are like, "What?"

Robin looks at me. I'm like, "That's what they do."

**El Morya:** Mmhmm.

**Mom:** It's normal for me, I don't care. Pfff. Everybody's thrown me off since the day I was born. Pfff. This is not anything not normal for me. I've been rejected since the day I was born on the planet.

I was like, "Fine, and I'm Mother Earth. And guess what? I have a counter plan against you fucking motherfuckers who went against Mother Earth and fuck you."

**Gabriel:** Get 'em, Mama.

**Mom:** How dare you even decide that you had power over Mother Earth's healing?

**Gabriel:** Huh. Wow. Fuckers. That's what's going to get 'em, it's going to be their downfall.

**Mom:** Exactly. Because how can you--and of course, it's all everywhere, "I'm going to justify this." I'm like, "Fuck off. I don't fucking want to hear your justification. What did you do to serve love? Period."

And it's action. It's not fucking wishy-washy, fucking mush. Suckysucky, game of sucking. Alright, fucking suck your own game or create it on yourself because I'm not in it. It's not my sucky-sucky game. I support love everywhere present.

**Gabriel:** Yup.

**Mom:** I watch these fucking people. Like, they have no idea what it is to serve love. To really serve love, it's through the food, it's through the food. It's service, music, atmosphere, everything.

I gave Philadelphia this fucking Gordon Ramsay shit. Someone asked me, like, "Are you Gordon Ramsay?" And I'm like, "Yes."

**Group:** [Laughter]

**Mom:** Because everything he says is exactly what I would say. There's nothing--

I'm so fucking brilliant. I was beyond my own brilliance. My parents couldn't understand it. I couldn't understand it but I kept going. Like, "Who are you?" I'm like, "Hmm. Looks like I'm God, parents. It's a possibility here that I'm God. Do you guys get it?"

They're like, pfff, gone. They didn't want to fucking hear that shit. "Oh, my daughter is God." It rolled around out there. They're like,

"Oh my daughter is not God, no. She couldn't possibly be that." My dad's like, rolling around and he's like, "But she is. She's God."

I'm like, "Alright." I'm just roaming around Dallas, everyone's like, "Who are you?" I'm like, "I don't know. What are you going to call me? God? Possibly." [Laughter] I thought it was funny as shit.

**Gabriel:** [Laughter] That is funny.

**Mom:** I didn't even care. I was like, "Pfff." And then they're just like, "Are you God?" I'm like, "Yeah. I am."

**Gabriel:** Yes, you are.

**Pam:** Yeah.

**Mom:** I just tell them the truth, you know? My dad was taking me around to multi-millionaires. I imagined that they would catch on, but they really didn't. They had no concept of anything, they were far gone. There was no way I could get to them. It was like, "Shit, fuck."

I'm fucking in Wonderland of myself, trying to help my dad. He's in Wonderland. I'm like, "We're fucking in Wonderland helping oil companies."

I didn't even know what I was doing. I was in the middle of it because I was grateful for helping, but my dad had it all. Like, shit. It was like, "What the fuck's going on?" And he's the vice president of the oil companies across Oklahoma, Texas, like everything. I'm trying to keep up with my dad.

**Gabriel:** Thank you, Daddy Reed [Mother God's earth step-father].

**El Morya:** Thank you, Daddy Reed.

**Mom:** Yeah, Daddy Reed. He was getting job offers left and right. Everyone wanted my dad because he was so grand.

So, the oil companies were hiring him left and right. Like, we are president, the president.

My dad was constantly consulting me, like, "Okay, they want me to be the president of this company." And then I'm like, "Okay, let me look at it. Let me look if it's the highest." And I would tell them a lot of times like, "No, it's not the highest, daddy. They're lying. They're fucking lying in our face, dad, and we have to realize what's going on."

I tried to tell him. He got caught up in the system. And for me to share whole organic truth information, he totally cut me off. I was like, "Okay, I'm done then. There's nothing I can do."

And then he died because he wasn't operating in his capacity. It was ridiculous for me. I was like, "Daddy, that's stupid." I mean, there was no reason, he knew exactly what I was doing. He had every information. It was absolutely ridiculous that he would be like, "Hey, stop your information." I was like, "Oh, fuck, that's not a good daddy." I told him and then he died.

**Gabriel:** Bring on me, Daddy Reed.

**Mom:** He was like, "Fine, I didn't do it." I'm like, "No, you didn't."

So yeah, 2015 came, my mom calls me. She's like, "You know Daddy Reed died?" I'm like, "Yeah, he's right here with me. I'm not alone with Daddy Reed right here."

**Group:** [Laughter]

**Mom:** She's like, "Can you tell him 'Hi' for me?" I was like, "Okay, mom. Pretty sure I can tell him 'Hi' for you." Pfff. Dumb.

**Group:** [Laughter]

**Mom:** She's like, "Well, he died." I'm like, "No, he didn't, he's still alive, mom."

**El Morya:** [Laughter] He's alive and well. Doing well.

**Mom:** Fucking whore. She's like, "Well, you know how much daddy did for you." I'm like, "Oh my God."

**El Morya:** [Laughter] Really?

**Mom:** Do you have to share with me, though? She's like, "You know how much daddy did for you." I'm like, "Okay, whose daddy?" First of all, I was like, "What are you saying, mom? Whose daddy? Daddy Reed for me is my daddy that came to my aid in life, in journey, and said I'm here for you. Who's your fucking dad?"

**Gabriel:** Who's your daddy?

**Mom:** She didn't even know what the fuck was going on. I was like, "That must be my whore, called my mother." Fucking dumbass bitch. Shit.

**Group:** [Laughter]

**Mom:** I had all plays going on. My sisters are like, "Are you talking to mother?" I'm like, "No, she's a whore." Our mother was a fucking bitch-ass whore, was a taker beyond. I was watching the whole thing. I was like, "You want to? Here's me, I'm the fucking giver."

I've got a whole family I'm watching. I'm like, "The fuck are you doing? Are you takers?" I had weapons of mass destruction against them. I used 'em. I was like, "Fuck off whores!" Blow 'em up. I'm like, "Who's left?"

And then my sisters would appear. I'm like, "Wow, that's funny." Sisters which I put in the programming. I'm like, "Go after them, just go." And then they report back and like, "Yeah, we did."

I'm like, "Yay!" which wasn't actually true because they fucking didn't do nothing. Then I realized, after doing all my reports, I'm like, "They fucking did nothing, fucking whores lied!" I'm like, "Okay, I have to deal with this." In universal law, I have to deal [pronounced similar to "dill"].

Robin's like, "Dill? What did you just say? Dill? Dill pickles?" Well, just shut the fuck up.

Anyway, this is me and Robin in there. Dill pickles, somewhere. I don't know what the fuck he's talking about, but dill pickles. Somehow, I landed in dill pickles.

Robin's been around for five years and now he's running on dill pickles. And I can hear--you can hear it? It's fucking running on dill pickles.

It just fucking hit me with, like, "Come on." I'm like, "What the fuck, you fucking come on, you fucking whore bitch." That's what I got.

I don't even know what the fuck you're talking about, Robin. Fucking whore bitch, that's what I got. You and me, we can fucking go at it. Fuck it, how many fucking ways--

**El Morya:** What's this? Are these dill pickles? Oh my. [Laughter]

**Gabriel:** [Laughter] Are these dill pickles? Is this manifestation?

**Mom:** [Laughter] Poor Robin is like, "Kick him in the ass!"

**El Morya:** Watched *The Matrix* too many times. [Laughter]

**Gabriel:** Holy shit!

**Mom:** Robin was coming straight at him and he was like--

**Gabriel:** You're going to get the kangaroo foot, boy! [Laughter]

**Mom:** He's like, "Got it, got it!" That's pretty cool.

I have circus animal people. They see the show. I'm like, "Is this a circus?" Everyone was like, "Yeah." I'm like, "Okay." I just lay back, like, "Circus. I'm in a circus." I love the circus, maybe that'll hold me and I'll hopefully, gracefully accept that, but I do.

Came to Crestone, fuck you, motherfuckers. And they all challenge me every moment. Challenge me if I could stay here or not. I'm like, "Who's here?"

I won. And they can fucking fuck off. And the town of Crestone's like, "Shit, she won." Yup, I won.

My fourth time going back. Nobody wants to come to Crestone. [Laughter]

"Are you going to Crestone?"

"Yeah."

"Okay, we're not going."

[Laughter] No one go to Crestone! It's fascinating that I had to travel so far.

**El Morya:** Jesus!

**Mom:** Come back, they're literally like, "Who are you?" I'm like, "God. And this is my town, you fucking motherfuckers."

And they're fucking running like banshees to be safe from your stupidity out there.

But I am safe. I understand, I know that completely. I'm producing the energy that is safe--

**Gabriel:** Yup, thank you, Mom.

**Mom:** --for all dimensions. I'm working hard a little bit. [Laughter] I got it.

**Gabriel:** Yes, you do!

**Pam:** Yeah!

**Mom:** I have to just stretch the energy out because it comes in and I just have to have enough energy to spread it out of my body and stuff. What a challenge, because it's there. If they harm it then I'm challenged.

I have to be vulnerable and let every atom know that Mother is available. It's challenging for me but I know how to manage it. I know how to deal with it. And that's the part of Crestone that they don't understand because they never take responsibility for anything.

**Gabriel:** White trash.

**Mom:** I'm like, "Know what? I take responsibility for everything." How about that, apples, atoms, and everybody on this planet? I take responsibility – full responsibility – for everything.

Right, wrong, whatever. I don't really care. Love has a deep foundation on this planet.

Fuck, fuck, fuck. I'm like, "Okay, no. It's no good"

**Gabriel:** Love Has Won!

**Mom:** Love. Angels. Dumb. Move away. Go.

# XVIII

## GOD'S PROPHECY
## OF BEING IN A HUMAN FORM

### 37.9964° N, 105.6997° W

*"Have a glass of wine, drink a beer, have a shot of tequila.*
*Who cares? And why not? Who made up those fucking rules?"*

## NOVEMBER 6, 2019

**LOVE BEINGS:** Mother of All Creation, Father of All Creation, Archeia Aurora, Archeia Hope, Buddha, Archangel Gabriel

**SCENE:** Sitting at a table surrounded by Hope and Aurora, with Father, Buddha, and Gabriel behind the camera, Mother joins the daily morning livestream.

---

**Group:** Good morning! [Cheering]

**Aurora:** [Motions to Mom] As you can see, we have a special guest today. [Laughter]

**Buddha:** In all of creation!

**Mom:** Where's my wine?

**Hope:** [Hands a glass of wine to Mom]

**Mom:** I'm a wino. Cheers, trolls! It's six o'clock, cheers!

**Group:** [Laughter]

**Mom:** Totally against our rules. That means fucking shut up, whore. There's no rules in heaven, get it? [Laughter]

**Buddha:** Get 'em. [Laughter]

**Mom:** Angel's like, "She's talking!" Yeah, actually, I'm talking. After moments of silence in hell. [Takes a drink] Good thing you guys didn't go all the way down there, you wouldn't have fucking made it.

**Buddha:** Nope.

**Mom:** You'd be, like, dead. Like, after one second, you'd be like, "Done." [Laughter] My fucking ass goes there with Germain. We're like, "We got this, right?"

"Actually, I don't." He's like, "We do!" I'm like, "No. Oh God." I'm talking to myself, I don't got this. He's like, "Yes, you do."

And actually, we did. Went all the way down to the depths of hell. I was like, "This is fun, mmhmm." Actually not. [Laughter] It's called hell for some reason. Why would you call it hell, the fucking most insane, chaotic, discourse, dysfunctional energy possible in creation?

**Father:** Dirty stuff.

**Mom:** Nothing like me. Go ahead, Adam, take us away.

[Musical interlude while Adam plays a song]

Everyone's excited. Good morning, Vietnam! [Laughter]

Always someone out there: "You're drinking? It's six o'clock, you must be a drunk." You know what? That's my favorite label. [Laughter] Cheers!

"Who is God? Pfff. God doesn't swear, God doesn't drink, God doesn't eat food" – that's about right. [Laughter] I'm only drinking. It saved my life, literally, though. [Holds up a glass of wine] If I didn't have this, I'd be dead. I wouldn't have made it, toast.

Yes, talk about stealing your joy. That's what everyone did. I'm still here, though. God. [Laughter] "What'd she say? She's God?" Yeah, and what? What you got? Are you God, too? Yup. [Laughter]

It was like, "You talk to dead people?" Yeah, I talk to dead people all my life. It's been my life talking to dead people, including Robin.

Robin's like, "I'm not dead." He's not dead, I swear to God. He's, like, cracking up, he's like, "That was good." [Laughter]

"Where's that crazy lady from the video?" That's what they're looking for. Shout out to Angela and daughter, we love you, our hearts go out.

**Buddha:** Love you, Angela. Thank you for everything.

**Mom:** We're with you and everyone who's going through their stuffies. [Laughter] I've had the most stuffies. Stuffies is a word, transform that shit. I'm like, "Got it." That's what everyone else has to do, too. It's all shit. Past, future, it's all shit. Crap doesn't even exist, just the Present Moment of Now. Have a glass of wine, drink a beer, have a shot of tequila. [Laughter] Who cares? And why not? Who made up those fucking rules?

**Aurora:** The Cabal.

**Mom:** Stupid dummies. "You can't do this." I'm like, "What? Who said that?" If someone said I can't do something, I was like, "I'm better sure that I was going to make sure that I did." That was that. [Laughter] You said I couldn't do it, oh, that means I will.

**Hope:** You don't follow the illusionary rules.

**Mom:** Magic words for God. What'd you say? I can't do--what did you say? Oh, that means I'm going to do it grander, that's what that is.

What's our title [of the livestream]? The event? I don't know, the prophecy?

**Hope:** Mom knows about that because she is it.

**Mom:** Yeah, just a little bit.

**Hope:** Just a little bit, just all of them. She's awesome.

**Mom:** Just about shoving my face like, what? I don't even know about prophecies. Angel's like, "Hmmm."

Okay, what? I'm who? Homo-say-what? [Laughter] Denied. Denied. They're like, "You're God." I'm like, "Denied. I am not." They're like, "Yes, you are." Great. What does that mean? I sat by a tree, contemplated like Buddha. [Takes a drink]

**Buddha:** Mama God! [Laughter]

**Mom:** Gotcha! I'm good. Right, Buddha?

**Buddha:** Yes, the best. [Laughter]

**Mom:** 16 live [streamers]. Anne-Marie, one of my biggest lovers, givers out there. Anne-Marie, thank you for my peppermint oil. [Laughter] Grateful. Peppermint saves me and then I got peppered out. And I was like, "There's too much peppermint!"

**Hope:** It's true.

**Mom:** Everyone's like, putting peppermint on me, trying to stop the processes, which we can't stop, right? You just have to go through it.

Peppermint was definitely my savior, also Velveeta Kraft cheese sandwiches. [Laughter] Robin saved my life because when I want to eat, "Eat this!" Fine, I'll eat the grilled cheese because I love it. [Laughter]

**Aurora:** You'd be surprised what has powered this ascension.

**Hope:** Right? Stuff you wouldn't fathom.

**Mom:** One of the moments was cream cheese. He's like, "Stuff it in your mouth." And I'm going to puke. He's like, "Just eat it. Actually, fuck, put some weight on you, it's like you're anorexic."

I'm like, "Ahhh!" He's like, "Bag of bones!" Oh shit, Robin. Bag of bones. It came down to this. I'm like, I didn't know what he was talking about at first-- [Reacts to noise off-camera] What was that?!

**Hope:** Drake [Toddler resident of Mission House].

**Mom:** Oh! [Laughter]

I didn't know what he was talking about at first. I'm like, "I'm a bag of bones?" Like, yeah. Then I saw Minnie Driver. I'm like, "Holy fuck." I was like, "Oh, that's like, anorexic, that's scary." [Laughter]

Never in my experience – this lifetime – to be that, and yeah, it's an experience going from a normal average 145 pounds to this morning 96.4--

**Group:** Wow.

**Mom:** --which I wasn't very happy about. Nor was Robin, nor were the Galactics. [Singing] "Wasting away in Margaritaville..." [Laughter] They're going to love that.

Okay, where's my comments? Come on. [Laughter]

I love you guys so I'm not crying today. It's good because normally I would be. I cry most days in my life for the moment.

So, let's talk about ascension. [Laughter]

**Gabriel:** Get 'em, Mom. Get 'em good.

**Mom:** [Hears a child making noise off-camera] They're coming in here, as they should. [Laughter] We have a visitor, it's called yelling. [Laughter] And our title is? [Takes a drink]

**Aurora:** "The Prophecy God."

**Mom:** Oh yes, that's right, I forgot. So, Present Moment of Now, everything just...yep, that's what it takes to be present. [Laughter]

Hey! Angels are on it, bring it on. [Lights a cigarette] Actually, that's what's happening, it's called Bring It On Day.

**Buddha:** Yeah!

**Mom:** Just bring it on, bring it up, let it go. Easier that way, trust me. I did it. First, I would know. It's a fucking shithole. But I did it so I can make an easier passageway for all of you guys.

**Group:** Thank you, Mama! [Applause]

**Mom:** It's my honor, it's my dedication, my love. And Saint Germain, and for me, my goal was to reach all 8+ billion people. I stated it in 2007 when I first came out to share about this energy that was coming. The prophecies, everything was being revealed to me. I had no idea and I was involved. I was like, "I was going to find that person. That person must be out there somewhere. I'll find him or her." And it was myself! Ding!

I went on some tangent. I had some other thing that's gone, damnit.

Angels! Angels all around, seriously. They'll pop crackle and roll. [Laughter] That's a good one, "Pop, crackle, and roll." Oh, yeah. [Laughter]

[Takes a drink] Let's talk about the prophecies, how it began in 2007. I mean, the Mission, actually. They're like, "Alright, you're God, so you got to go on Mission." I'm like, "Oh, fuck. Everybody's God, I'm not the only one, am I?" [Laughter] I was looking around like, "Oh shit, am I the only one that knows? Okay, weird. Yeah, I'm in a land where nobody remembers they are God besides me, great. I can do this, I got this."

And I was like, I told the angels, like, "Everyone's going to hate me because I'm saying I'm God, they don't like God. Can I say a different name?" They're like, "No." Okay! Then I'll just fucking come out. "Hi! I'm Mother God, cheers."

**Group:** [Applause]

**Mom:** Prophecies revealed. Who's coming? Jesus. Surprise! Surprise! I actually was Jesus, to my surprise, to myself.

I always was like, all my life, "I'm God." They're like, "Shut up, I don't know what you're talking about." I wasn't fucking Jesus. Somebody else was Jesus. I'll find that person. Looking, looking. You're supposed to be here, I'll find them.

**Father:** A big party. [Laughter]

**Mom:** And the day the angels told me, they're like, "You were Jesus." I'm like, "No, I wasn't." Like, "Yes, you were."

I'm like, "Hey, Jesus was a man." They're like, "No." I'm like, "What do you mean, no?" They're like, "Jesus was a woman."

Jesus was a woman?! Interesting. They fucking lied to me! Whores! Ding dong! Who was Jesus? Me. Who's God? Me. Angels got me in one whole swoop of 10 years. [Laughter] 10 years!

"Do you remember?" Nope. I don't know shit, I don't remember shit, I don't know shit, I don't even know what the fuck's going on. And somehow, I'm involved. [Laughter] I didn't even know that. I was just an outsider looking in and then all of a sudden, I'm the star of the show. I'm like, "Wow, that's cool."

Prophecies! Actually, I let the angels take it away, what you got? [Laughter]

I do want to re-heart everybody: I like little gifts. I even like little words, money, and all that. They're resources to me. They fuel the Mission, they fuel us all to continue to serve love everywhere present. And little gifts I have on the wish list on Amazon, they're five dollars. Are you kidding me? That's a cup of coffee.

**Father:** She's God, cheapskates. [Laughter]

**Mom:** Yeah, I don't ask for, like, "I'm asking for five billion dollars." And I'll build a Crystal School for the children. I support love everywhere present. If you're not giving to that, those who support love everywhere present, you're serving a black hole, period. Go ahead shove it in, out. If you are serving love, it comes right back to you. You give me a five-dollar gift, I give you a million dollars, how about that?

**Hope:** It's a good trade.

**Mom:** That's a good trade.

**Father:** You're pretty good.

**Mom:** In energies, it's so simple, energetic-wise. Those who serve love energetically serve the greatest good of all, for the greatest good of all, for all of us. And that's who you support. What are you doing supporting EGO?

EGO is not for anybody. EGO is for itself, self-importance, taker, taker, taker. And takers don't go to heaven, by the way, just so you know. They're not going to like that one.

Givers, on the other hand, givers inherit Planet Earth, and I will give everything to the givers. I guarantee that. It's already got it, but the givers who are hiding behind bushel baskets and all that shit, you better stand up now or else you'll just be a taker, you go to Taker Land. No Fun Land over there. Heaven's fun, you guys want to go to heaven?

**Aurora:** Yeah.

**Mom:** [Takes a drink] I am so grateful that all the trolls have disengaged back down. I'm grateful. I'm so grateful.

**Father:** Back in their hole.

**Mom:** Yeah. I like that though. That way, they don't have to face me and get real. That's the whole thing about the EGO on this planet, is that they were afraid to face what was real. I'm EGO's – should I say this?

**Aurora:** Robin's gonna probably tell you to say it.

**Hope:** Yeah, Robin's probably going to be, "Say it!"

**Mom:** Yeah, you know, EGOs don't like me. [Laughter] They just don't like love, they don't like laughter.

My daddy, we got kicked out of restaurants all the time. "She's laughing out loud!" And this is a problem, obviously. Humanity are like, "She's laughing! It's making us nervous! Please shut her up!" My dad was like, "Yeah, you shut up. You guys shut the fuck up. My daughter will laugh, enjoy, and EGOs back the fuck down."

It's not your planet. You took over, like whores, and you destroyed my planet. You made everyone dysfunctional. Look what you did!

Yeah, I'm so proud. [Laughter] Yeah, we're killing each other over here. I kill you, I kill you, we're at war. Love has nothing like that. There's no war. Love marrying love is the original blueprint. Original blueprint for this planet, and that's returning now.

**Buddha:** Yeah!

**Hope:** Oh yeah!

**Mom:** And love's in charge.

**Group:** [Applause]

**Mom:** And no EGO. Edging God Out. You listen to Wayne Dyer, anybody? 6:30 am, 11 percent.

**Father:** Happy birthday.

**Buddha:** Yeah, happy birthday.

**Mom:** Alright, you guys talk, go ahead.

**Hope:** [Gestures to Mom] So, everybody, this is God. You didn't know, now you know.

**Mom:** No! [Laughter]

**Hope:** We'll keep it a secret. [Laughter]

**Mom:** I'm not on the planet. No one told you I was coming at all. [Laughter] Look at the prophecies: God is coming, God is coming.

"Oh, God's here!"

"No, she's not."

**Hope:** No? Crap.

**Mom:** The prophecy lied? The prophecy's not true?

**Buddha:** Great spirit!

**Mom:** "Jesus is going to appear out of the sky and save us!" [Laughter] Right? "Kiss my ass," that's what I said. [Lights a cigarette] Jesus is not going to save your ass.

**Hope:** You have to save yourself.

**Mom:** You can save your own soul by choosing love, the same word as God, and truth. God. Love. Truth. Same word, everybody.

What's your problem? You got a problem with truth? You have a problem with love? You have a problem with God? Obviously, fucking EGO whores. They're the only ones that have problems, EGOs on this planet. And actually, EGOs don't exist, nobody in creation has an EGO except who? Humanity.

**Hope:** How you like them apples?

**Mom:** Humanity has something creation hasn't. We look at like, "What the fuck is that? What're they doing?" I have to be the buffer, like, "I have no idea. They're doing this, someone said this, who the fuck knows."

**Gabriel:** Homo-say-what?

**Mom:** Homo-say-what? [Laughter] What?

**Hope:** There are even books out there, guys, that say the EGO is humanity's problem, right? Mom's not the only one talking about it. Wayne Dyer [Deceased motivational speaker] talked about it, that's how she figured it out.

**Mom:** Wayne Dyer was my inspiration, by the way. He told me, like, "Here's the problem: It's called E-G-O." I'm like, "What the fuck is that? E-G-O? Okay. E-G-O. Edging God Out? Oh! That's the EGO!"

That's their fucking problem, no wonder they can't fucking hear me, duh! Got it! Thank you, Wayne. Wayne's with me, by the way, if anyone wants to know.

And anyone out there who put out about EGO and Wayne, he's fucking pissed, not happy. You should have a healthy EGO? Fuck that shit. You can't have a fucking healthy EGO and the EGO is fucking shit. You can't turn a piece of shit into wonder sun. Good luck, try it. Actually, I probably did in my experiments and it didn't work. I'm pretty sure I tried it.

**Hope:** You tried serving them for 14 years.

**Mom:** Yeah, serve your EOGs as I'm throwing up. Now I'm withered away. Oops. Didn't mean to do that, but I had to do what I had to do in service to love and humanity. Robin's been telling me all day to forgive them. Like, I don't want to. I don't want to.

**Hope:** Who would want to? Nobody out there would do it.

**Mom:** When you're fucking assassinated 556 times by humanity? I forgive you, that's good. But I do, and I take full responsibility on top of that, to transform it into love everywhere present.

And that's a real being, who everybody is in their soul. These fucking programmed EGO minds, fucking whores. I had to study that fucking bitch. I don't want to look at it anymore. Done. Done with programmed EGOs.

**Hope:** Bye.

**Mom:** Bye. Robin's telling me to exit.

**Aurora:** Thank you so much.

**Hope:** We love you.

**Mom:** You're welcome.

**Hope:** Mother God, everybody.

**Gabriel:** Get 'em, Mama!

**Buddha:** Mama God! And Pops!

**Group:** Thank you, Mama! We love you!

# XIX

## Happy Spins-Giving

### 37.9964° N, 105.6997° W

*"I am disclosure, my body is disclosure, my body is a starship, and I have all of creation with me. Kiss my ass."*

## NOVEMBER 28, 2019

**LOVE BEINGS:** Mother of All Creation, Father of All Creation, Archeia Hope, Archeia Aurora, Buddha, Archangel Gabriel
**SCENE:** Sitting at a table surrounded by Hope and Aurora, with Buddha and Gabriel behind the camera, Mother joins the daily morning livestream. She is eventually joined by Father.

---

**Group:** [Cheering]

**Buddha:** Mama God!

**Mom:** Thank you. Happy Thanksgiving.

[Speaking to a dog] There's Pebbles! Thank you, Pebbles. Good girl, you're such a good girl, along with the other bad puppies.

**Group:** [Laughter]

**Mom:** Okay, feet up. It's alright. Mommy's okay.

[Speaking to the group] She's concerned.

**Hope:** Yeah she's--

**Mom:** Good morning everybody!

**Group:** [Cheers]

**Buddha:** Mama God!

**Mom:** [Presses a toy button on desk]

**Toy Button:** [Plays recorded voice] "Woah, watch your step! You just walked into some bullshit!"

**Group:** [Laughter]

**Mom:** Watch that step! They have no idea what's coming next. It's scary!

**Hope:** [Laughter] It's scary!

**Aurora:** Spooked!

**Mom:** I've been spooked.

**Hope:** Yeah, you're spooked. [Laughter]

**Mom:** I've been spooked at myself.

**Group:** [Laughter]

**Mom:** Damn it. Let me smoke a cigarette. [Laughter] And it's a cigarette! [Holds a cigarette up to the camera] Yeah, it's laced with something!

**Group:** [Laughter]

**Mom:** No, no.

**Gabriel:** Yeah, Mom!

**Mom:** But actually, the real people love me and know me, and why would they fuck me? There's no need. Love, God, same-same. Who's scared? EGOs! [Laughter]

Go study Ian. He told me about it. He was like, "This is what they're going to do." As the ethics train came upon the fucking power train, he said, "Fuck you bitch, move over." EGOs are in fucking fight/flight, we're in the middle of it.

Happy Thanksgiving. Thanksgiving is my most favorite holiday, not only because of the weather. [Sings] The fall...

**Group:** [Laughter]

**Mom:** Grateful that I breathe, leave your nose. So I sing the song *Nobody Knows It But Me* because you don't fucking know.

I woke up this morning with eight million EGOs in my face. I'm like, "Happy Thanksgiving!" I'm like, "Oh no, there's no Happy Thanksgiving for me. There's no happy. No happy. Fight."

Happiness and love and true giving and living on this planet organically, instead of fake figures, pretenders, and...I'm not going to, I'm not gonna go into whatever Robin's got me saying. He's got me for the past six hours, in my face.

How about having your guy's Robin Williams in your face for six hours? Not like every day he's in my face. Anyways. [Laughter] Bypass. Robin Williams in your face. Wouldn't have to deal with everybody's hate. Towards what? Not to his God. Push yourselves.

Today is the moment to say thanks to your Creator and to yourselves. Because if you're still alive right now...

**Aurora:** Thank Mom!

**Hope:** Yeah, thank Mom!

**Group:** [Cheers]

**Mom:** I'm still alive. And this dress showed up out of nowhere, I'm like--

**Aurora:** We've never seen this dress ever.

**Mom:** Never seen the dress out of--I don't even wear brown.

Robin's like, "Okay." Yeah, that's called angel magic.

And Robin Williams up all of our asses, not including--he's up mine, but he's going to be up all of our asses to get into right action to natural organic evolution. With it, Happy Thanksgiving.

[Speaking to Father] Father?

**Father:** Yes?

**Group:** [Laughter]

**Mom:** You want to say anything? Father God!

**Hope:** Oh yeah, yeah!

**Group:** [Cheers]

**Buddha:** Father God!

**Father:** Thank you. Just wanted to reiterate, children, what Mother said about this being the day to thank your Creator. That's what today is, we're giving thanks for life. Life and all the beautiful things that life has to offer. All the love that we have to offer.

**Mom:** Get 'em.

**Father:** We all feel it in every heartbeat. We all feel it as we gaze into each other's eyes throughout our mornings, our afternoons, through our evenings.

We feel that one connection that we all share through our smiles, that glimmer of life and hope in our eyes. We all share connected to Mother God, the oneness. We feel this more as we get into the holidays. Thank you, Mom.

**Mom:** This day is also very dear to me because my birthday...

**Hope:** Yeah, two days. [Laughter]

**Mom:** Is that two days?

**Hope:** Mmhmm. Two days.

**Mom:** Great.

**Group:** [Cheers]

**Mom:** Where's my parrots?

**Group:** [Laughter]

**Aurora:** Where's the motherfucking parrots?!

**Hope:** Yeah, where are the fucking parrots?

**Mom:** They better be safe.

**Hope:** They're alive. They have food and water, too.

**Mom:** Okay. Better be.

**Hope:** Yup.

**Group:** [Laughter]

**Mom:** I'm totally concerned about my parrots. I don't got lots--

**Hope:** But your parrots are coming.

**Mom:** --but I got parrots.

**Group:** [Laughter]

**Hope:** And chubby goldfish.

**Mom:** And chubby goldfish, and I got him. [Points to Father God]

**Group:** [Laughter]

**Mom:** We got Pebbles and two puppies, Sebastian and Flimsy. [Laughter] She just flims around.

**Hope:** Like a deer on ice.

**Mom:** Yes. I swear she was, like, from a deer.

**Hope:** Yeah, she is.

**Mom:** I'm grateful every moment. In the back of my brain, I'm in constant meditation and gratefulness. Gratitude for love, for life. No, I don't want to be here anymore. No one in my condition, in the state I'm in, would.

No way you guys could fucking make it, that's why I did it, so I can withstand the amount of energy to take on the physical ascension. So, do I have to reveal that? Yes, of course. I am disclosure, my body is disclosure, my body is a starship, and I have all of creation with me. Kiss my ass. [Holds up her middle finger to the camera]

**Group:** [Cheers]

# XX

## GOD'S MOST RECENT VISIT TO SHARE HER STORY

### 37.9964° N, 105.6997° W

*"I don't know shit, I don't know what's going on, but I choose love every moment and that's the key. As long as you choose love, you're always going the right direction. Always."*

## DECEMBER 16, 2019

**LOVE BEINGS:** Mother of All Creation, Father of All Creation, Archeia Hope, Archeia Aurora, Buddha, Archangel Gabriel
**SCENE:** Sitting at a table surrounded by Hope and Aurora, with Buddha and Gabriel behind the camera, Mother joins the daily morning livestream. She is eventually joined by Father.

---

**Hope:** Get 'em. Woo!

**Group:** [Applause]

**Buddha:** Mama God!

**Mom:** Well, I just wanted to – that's beautiful, FM – share that story. The holy grail story was pretty big because it was December 7th, in 2007. [Laughter] You're like, "Holy shit!"

My whole moment was for my son, that moment, to watch *The Wizard of Oz* for the first time. And I had set up this dinner and I was waiting for it. I was like, "We're gonna watch this!"

We watched a lot of movies together without me having to document from the angels. And this particular – as soon as the movie started – the angels were like, "Pick up your notebook!" I'm like, "Oh shit! Okay! What the fuck is going on? I'll document. What are you saying?"

And that particular time I was documenting everything. I was like, "Holy shit, that's why my aunt dressed me up as Dorothy." A 14-year-old girl out there in Orange County, California.

She was a Broadway designer of clothes and she was like, "No, you're Dorothy." I'm like, "Wow!" I had a basket with the Toto dog and the dress. [Laughter] She's like, "Knock on the door!" of all these freaking mansion houses. I'm like, "Nothing? I'm Dorothy." [Laughter]

And I always teased everybody about if you take the map of the whole United States and if you put an X in them, there's me, that's where I was born. I even would walk to the park where this — and I'm mostly what, what am I, Robin? 43% Cherokee Indian.

So, there was this Indian statue that was in the middle of town and I would always walk to it and I would stare at it. I'm like, "What does it say? X marks the spot, huh? Interesting." [Laughter]

What does that mean? Roses and vine things. I was like, "Dee daa lee...smell the roses." [Laughter] X marks the spot.

[Notices a dog] Who's that? Oh, Mimzy. Watch my feet, love. Watch Mommy's feet, thank you. Good girl. She's like, "Oh my gosh, she's ice cold." Aww, good girl. Surrender!

We have another special song Adam's working on, excited about that.

So, the part of the story went, so all of a sudden, the angels were like, they had me document, "You have the red slippers and nobody can take them from you." I was like, "Okay. What the fuck does that mean?"

And then it was on TBS. If anyone remembers TBS, or I don't know if it's still out there…

**Hope:** It is.

**Mom:** But they would have their little questions and then they would have answers after. So, I wrote that down. Two minutes later, TBS comes on and says, "What do the movie slippers mean?" I'm like, "What?! What the fuck?!" [Laughter]

Okay, so, I was tripping. I was like, "The fuck is going on? What do the ruby slippers represent?" And I just wrote down, "You have the red sl--." I was watching every commercial, I was like, "Oh my God, this is getting too long! Get on with it, please tell me."

**Aurora:** [Laughter] Please tell me what it means!

**Mom:** I'm sweating. *Blues Clues!* Who the fuck am I? [Laughter]

And the answer comes on, the ruby red slippers mean the holy grail. I was like, "What? What does that mean? I'm the holy grail?" I was like, "Okay, write that down. I don't know what it means." [Laughter]

I didn't know half of what the angels were trying to tell me. I just write it down. [Laughter] I'm like, "I'm confused, what are you telling me? I'm God? Everyone's God? I know this in my heart." They're like, "Um, well, you're the main God."

I'm just like, "Is there a main God?" [Laughter] So freaking gullible. That's one of my other names. My daddy always called me "Gullible."

I don't know shit, I don't know what's going on, but I choose love every moment and that's the key. As long as you choose love, you're always going the right direction. Always.

You can't make this stuff up, you guys. I mean, we should be the favorite channel on the whole planet right now. If you guys aren't spreading that...losers. [Laughter]

I think they came from Robin. I'm pretty sure I felt that energetically. I was like, "Uh oh." Robin in my face this morning, I'm like, "Oh great, we're in a battle." I threw him under the bus a couple of times.

Dragon! They probably don't understand that yet, they probably--they haven't seen it.

**Hope:** Maybe some moments last year.

**Mom:** I mean, well, maybe. Father, would you like to say anything?

**Father:** Sure. I was just screening back through the videos whether you had a dragon or not. And there was a couple I could recall. [Laughter]

**Hope:** [Laughter] That's exactly what you mean.

**Father:** What a great story Mom shared today about the holy grail.

**Mom:** It's one of our favorite stories.

**Father:** Yeah.

**Mom:** I was very shocked. And then sitting there waiting for the commercials, I was like, "What? What are they trying to tell me?" I love it!

**Father:** We were discussing how it pertains to this time and how the collective has essentially taken her feet out. And that's part of it, you know, they take the feet out--

**Mom:** Holy grail.

**Father:** --so that she can't put the ruby slippers on, so to say. It's just so stupid. So backwards.

**Mom:** Yeah, it's sad.

**Father:** Many events going on and keep the joy. Keep the joy 100%, children, for Mother. She created us that way. She's the one going through the experience and we're all grateful for that, eternally grateful. Always in support.

**Mom:** Yes.

**Father:** And that's what you kids can do out there, is be your divine selves. She said if you just choose love in every moment, everything's going to be fine.

We're so blessed to be here with you today. We're going to get Mom out of here now, so she can continue her ascension.

**Group:** [Applause]

**Gabriel:** Love you, Mama!

**Buddha:** Mama God!

**Mom:** I intend that we have more experiences with you guys. Just keep pushing for love.

# XXI

## MOTHER GOD'S MESSAGE TO HUMANITY

### 37.9964° N, 105.6997° W

*"And every one of you that went against me, you're going to get it!"*

## JULY 13, 2020

☆★★★★ 200 ★★★★☆

**LOVE BEINGS:** Mother of All Creation, Father of All Creation
**SCENE:** Perched on a deck outside her bedroom, Mother shares a message to the light-worker community while Father films.

---

**Mom:** Fucking...I was impressing every drunk on the planet as Marilyn Monroe. But besides that point... [Laughter]

**Father:** [Laughter] You were saying?

**Mom:** Yes. I commanded all my atoms to come home, back into the light. In order for them to come home back into the light, they had to be fucking whores. Bad to the bone.

[Counts on her fingers] Rape! Pillage! Thieves! Out of right action completely. Holy fucking shit!

You know I'm, like, eight billion EGOs? Yeah, I got this biiiitch. I got 'em, Robin! [Cheers]

**Father:** Woo!

**Mom:** Universal law! No matter what's happened to me, I will still stand for love, no matter what.

You can, like, fucking tear me down, fucking kill me. I've been killed several times. Kill me! Kill you!

**Father:** Kilroy!

**Mom:** Fucking EGO-programmed mind. You're fucking done! Cabal, over! Spiritual EGO whores, done! If you're not connected to me, you're out. Thank you for your service.

Connect in, done. If you're not…well, if you're not connected in, you're fucking done. You're all bitches.

**Father:** No go home.

**Mom:** Fucking whores.

**Father:** No "ET go home" for you, bitch whores.

**Mom:** Fucking battled me! My own lightworkers battled me! Serving love! And bringing a new paradigm, you fucking dick whores!

**Father:** [Laughter]

**Mom:** You're about to get it!

**Father:** Get 'em.

**Mom:** And every one of you that went against me, you're going to get it! Thank you.

# XXII

## TRANSMISSIONS FROM
## THE HAWAIIAN PORTAL

### 22.0964° N, 159.5261° W

*"You can do a runaround and fuck it, and fucking fucking fuck.
Whatever, I don't fucking care. Because I know in my heart, Santa Claus is me."*

### JULY 26, 2020

**LOVE BEINGS:** Mother of All Creation, Father of All Creation, Father of the Multi-verse

**SCENE:** Quarantined in their hotel room after arriving in Hawaii, Mother films special moments between herself, Father, and FM. Each transmission represents a different video shared with humanity, all from the same evening.

---

# [TRANSMISSION ONE]

**Father:** [Speaking to FM] ...what you can do to us. It's been well documented what you're capable of doing, not to only us, but the rest of the team.

**FM:** You're right. But what I meant was I wasn't trying to do that, but it happened unconsciously

**Mom:** [Lights a cigarette]

**Father:** But why are you unconscious?!

**FM:** I don't know, Father.

**Mom:** [Scoffs] You don't know? That's not your contract. Your contract is to be conscious. So, having the unconscious is saying, "I'm failing my contract, Mother." Let's get it straight, here.

**Father:** Say it!

**FM:** I'm failing my contract when I'm unconscious.

**Mom:** Don't--why are you looking to the left?

**Father:** That's his go-to.

**Mom:** Yeah.

**Father:** It's to look away from both Mother and Father.

**Mom:** [Speaking to FM] You have to look. What have you done?

**FM:** I've been out of integrity and failing my contract.

**Mom:** Why?! Tell us!

**FM:** Because the EGO-programmed mind hates God.

**Father:** And you are?

**FM:** A cockroach?

**Mom:** [Scoffs]

**Father:** The EGO-programmed mind!

**Mom:** The EGO-programmed mind.

**Father:** I mean, how dense can you be? I just basically said, "Repeat this." And you went to something else. And you're a whore. You know better. Even as being insulted, you have a better insult for yourself than God does. Do you notice it?

**FM:** [Nods]

**Father:** Okay. So, everything that you did is:

You interrupted and blocked Mom's videos so we can't re-heart what we were saying.

Simple commands were given before bed. We'll add, so the whole team knows, he fucked off the tea, never brought Mom tea.

Took her sandwich away, left it out on the cupboard.

And then stayed up for hours to suck from us so that...? What?

**FM:** Things could be in right action?

**Father:** [Laughter]

**FM:** [Shrugs] That's what I thought.

**Father:** So that it would appear to Mom that I had been sucking on her all night.

**FM:** That too.

**Father:** That too, okay. Thank you. And then upon getting up, then what happened?

**FM:** Then I was taking things personal from the start.

**Mom:** [Laughter] Okay.

**Father:** First thing you did was get up and sit in the dark. That's what I observed. I'm like, "Why isn't he putting a light on?" Because you love the dark. Who loves the dark? Cockroaches! Cockroaches love the dark so they can scuttle around, you can't see what the fuck they're doing. But then when the light came on...you see the pictures. [Points to photos on phone]

**Mom:** All lies.

**Father:** You must transform this now!

**Mom:** You have to. Don't take it personal.

**Father:** You turned it on yesterday, FM. But you know why you turned it on? 'Cause you stole the fucking energy from me.

**Mom:** Energy stealer!

**Father:** Yeah.

**Mom:** Caught ya, cockroach. "Cocky, cocky," says Robin.

**Father:** And then when you did it, then we went out and I was fucking drained. It's just, I watch you, it's unconscious.

**Mom:** That's a cock. Cock, cock! Cock-a-roo! [Laughter]

# [TRANSMISSION TWO]

**Father:** [Reading a text message from FM back to him] "I'll pay whatever, but I have limited cash." Listen to that half-assed whore statement. "I'll pay whatever, but I don't have whatever. So, I'm going to offer you minimum."

**Mom:** "I'll just give you half. I'll just give you half-ass God."

**Father:** Mmhmm. And take!

**Mom:** I'm like, "You know what? You can take your half-ass God and shove it up your fucking ass!" Shove it! Because I don't fucking need it. I don't want a half-ass God. That's not real.

Real God is whole, true, pure, always in integrity. There's no lying. There's no [makes puking noises]. Throw up! Liars! You wanna think in your beyond imaginations of Whoreland fantasies that I accept that that's true? You're fucking wrong.

Better fucking take that fucking bitch and throw it out. Because Santa Claus is real but Santa Claus doesn't exist in EGO-programmed minds, I'll tell you that.

You can do a runaround and fuck it, and fucking fucking fuck. Whatever, I don't fucking care. Because I know in my heart, Santa Claus is me. I have been shown that for so many years that I don't even know. But I have to sit here in fucking pain, suffering, as I present Santa Claus making all dreams come true.

And I sit here in terror as you guys, like, have a good time. I'm like, "What the fuck is this shit? Yeah, I'll do that. I'll fucking have, you know, a fucking Santa Claus moment." I'm Santa Claus.

You're gonna fucking get it because I am the real Santa Claus. And this is about to be really retarded as we show the ignorance.

I have a hurricane coming, Hurricane Douglas. Doo-ga-las, that's what I call it. It's called a doo-ga-las hurricane.

You're done, bitch. You're so done. Thank you.

# [TRANSMISSION THREE]

**Mom:** [Speaking to FM] Are you crying?

**FM:** I jumped on that call so quick because I wanted to get what you wanted, Mom. That's the way it was.

**Father:** [Speaking to FM] But it's not! She just said it, that it's what *you* wanted.

**Mom:** That's what you [FM] wanted!

**Father:** You're in denial and you're still putting it on her.

**Mom:** You're blaming me for your fucking fuckery.

**Father:** You [FM] keep looking over. [Points to a corner of the room]

**Mom:** Fuck off, bitch! Damnit. We're bringing out what is real and true because this is what I asked for. I want full disclosure. I'm full disclosure. I have nothing to hide.

What, you want me to take another tequila shot? I'll fucking do that shit. Bitch! Where's my tequila shot? Tequila shot! I got some tea.

**Father:** It's coming. I got it, I got it.

[Holds up a phone] They [FCGCT] sent a message. Stacy wants to take one of your blankets with your face on it on the plane. Aurora said, "No, you have to ask Mom first." She's trying to take your blanket, I guess.

**Mom:** Oh God.

**Father:** Emergency taker! Emergency taker!

**Mom:** Emergency! Alright. Stacy, she loves me so much.

**Father:** [Mocking Stacy] "I got to take her face!"

**Mom:** [Laughter]

**Father:** [Serves Mom a tequila shot]

**Mom:** Stacy, I love her. She wants to come to Hawaii to come cook. I observe her bravery for that.

**Father:** Yeah.

**Mom:** But she's going to fucking get it if she wants to come here. If you want to be in Mother and Father God's space, you better be fucking pure, true, and in integrity. And if not, better fucking get the fuck away. That is purity. Hilarion is showing this here.

[Speaking to FM] Hey, Hilarion, are you pure, pure whole integrity?

**FM:** I do my best.

**Mom:** [Scoffs]

**Father:** That's not the question.

**Mom:** That is not what we asked, that's not what we said!

**Father:** Holy shit!

**Mom:** You don't fucking do your best! You *are* your best. What the fuck are you talking about, you fucking whore?

Oh, roam around! Roam. I'll spin 'em.

**Father:** And then you [FM] walk away.

**FM:** You guys got me, I don't know what the fuck to do. I can't do anything.

**Mom:** What, what are you doing then? What, you can't do anything?

**Father:** [Laughter] "I can't!"

**Mom:** [Mocking FM] "I can't do anything for God 'cause I'm fucking dumb!"

**Father:** What are you doing, then, if you can't do anything?

**Mom:** Roaming around.

**Father:** Just roaming?

**Mom:** Yeah.

**FM:** I mean, I can't do anything without being picked apart.

**Father:** [Laughter]

**FM:** I half-assed the incense when I walked back to light it.

**Father:** You half-assed the incense after three years?

**Mom:** You half-ass everything. Tell humanity, "I am a half-ass." Are they half-assed, too?

**Father:** [Speaking to FM] What's with the hands in the pockets?

**Mom:** What the fuck is going on here?

**FM:** I don't know what to do with myself.

**Father:** [Laughter]

**FM:** I just want you to ascend and be happy.

**Father:** Maybe transform? That might be a good thing to do. Your contract?

**Mom:** It's called evolution, bitch. Evolution, bitches! Let's get it together. My feet don't work, but I will fucking work my ass off for evolution. Thank you.

# XXIII

## LET'S JUST SAY, WE GOT THIS

### 22.0964° N, 159.5261° W

*"I love you, but I can't love you if you are not loving yourself.*
*And I can't love you if you are hating me for absolutely nothing. What did I do? Nothing."*

## AUGUST 20, 2020

**SCENE:** Beginning on the beach in Hawaii, Mother and Father speak into the camera and share messages and updates with humanity. Eventually, they move into the house and continue the livestream from their bed.

**Mom:** Whoa.

**Father:** Get every moment for God.

**Mom:** Epic. Go back a thousand videos ago on my YouTube, I was fucked in the butt. They stole everything from me. And I'm still here. I'm still kicking butt! Thank you. I didn't back down from EGO's demands, fuck them.

**Father:** Just listen to her.

[Speaking to FM] Get 'em, FM!

**Mom:** [Laughter] Mer-man!

**Father:** He was the mer-man.

**Mom:** I don't know what is going on. I'm fucking live, though. According to Master Saint Germain and Master Robin Williams and Mer-man out there--there's Father.

**Father:** Hey!

**Mom:** We don't know what's going on at all, we have no idea, we're just working it. That's what we do as divine intelligent beings — you fucking work it into right action.

[Speaking to Father] What is he [FM] doing? Do not touch the bottom of the ocean! There are rocks out there! Okay, don't hit rocks. Oh, he just got caught by the wave!

**Father:** [Speaking to FM] What's up, fancy pants?

**Mom:** Fancy pants! How do you, oh, I have got four people here [on stream]. Like, oh yeah. And I might get on the phone. Why aren't they here? All the team is not here, nobody is. Isn't that disgusting to you?

**Father:** You know, what's more important is that you're here. Yes, it's disappointing. But at the same time, they don't want the miracles? Not gonna get the miracles.

**Mom:** Okay.

**Father:** We're gonna stay and stream some more. And the children that do show up, we're grateful to you, let you on the boat.

**Mom:** What?

**Father:** Coming to see you on a boat, right?

**Mom:** Which boat?

**Father:** There's boats coming with children on the boats.

**Mom:** Oh yeah, from Europe. [Laughter]

**Father:** Yes, they're coming to see you. See, if the kids here don't appreciate God, there's going to be kids all around the world that appreciate God, of course, and they're coming here by September 1st.

Because we have been pounding them night and day, night and day, because we love you. Through your darkest to lightest, we love you.

**Mom:** There's Trinity. Trinity is in there. I can't see the chat.

**Father:** Let me clean the screen for you.

**Mom:** Okay. So, the chat keeps disappearing.

**Father:** Okay, the technology is changing. I mean, I should give you my phone. That's your phone.

**Mom:** It's trying to, like, do some stuff. Whatever, whores.

**Father:** [Speaking to FM] You heard what I said? Mom's been on my phone. I'll take this phone. It's gonna send out 'cause it's the newest, get it? She should have the newest. Why do I have it? That's why I'm not even comfortable holding it. Give her that phone and everything programmed over to it. Know what I'm saying? 'Cause that's the one, that's the starship. You got it, son. Get it!

**Mom:** It's trying to do stuff I don't understand. Love you, Fathers. Anthony--

**Father:** Yeah, I called Anthony here last night. He's like, "No, I got kids, I can't go nowhere."

**Mom:** Okay. I wish it was. I pray every day. I have to get on medical beds immediately.

**Father:** Immediately.

**Mom:** I'm praying right now. Somehow, I deal with all the pain. I have no idea, it's fucking incredible.

You want to talk about incredibleness? Of dealing with an amount of pain that I can't describe? But nobody on this planet could even fucking handle whatsoever. But I got you, I got it all, and I wonder why.

I wonder, is this still recording? I don't know. Oh, there's ten people [watching the livestream].

My brain, like, stops. Like, "Oh, don't go there." I'm like, "I'm going because I gotta do it, no matter what. No matter what."

This stream is spinning and I don't really fucking give a shit.

[Speaking to Father] The clouds are coming in on me, everyone's spinning. If I get cold...I'm starting to. The sun is not coming out. There's a huge cloud right there. The sun is not coming out. I love the sun.

**Father:** I know, it's coming out. Give it a moment, the clouds move fast.

**Mom:** I don't want to be here.

**Father:** It's gonna move fast. It's gonna be okay. They don't want us on the beach 'cause what? 'Cause you'll heal.

**Mom:** That's a big cloud. It's all clouds.

**Father:** They don't want you on the beach 'cause you're healing. It's gonna be ok.

**Mom:** No, it's not.

[Group leaves the beach and returns to the house. Mother continues the livestream from her bed]

**Mom:** It's reconnecting.

**Father:** I ran it up for you as fast as I could.

**Mom:** Okay. Well, I only got like seven people. [Laughter] I can't believe that. You know what, Deepak Chopra can get more than that, holy shit. Oh my God, why? Why does everyone hate me?

**Father:** They're all complacent fucking assholes.

**Mom:** And I'm the most loving being of all! And I get fucking beat on and abused and whatever.

**Father:** They're complacent assholes! It's okay just to sit there and fuck it up.

**Mom:** You have to calm down, Father. It's true but we're all upset about this. It's retarded. I have fifteen people [streaming]? I'm God! We're all God, but I'm God and nobody is fucking listening because they fucking hate me?

**Father:** They hate her!

**Mom:** You have to feel into that and how disappointing that is for me. I love you, I love you, I love you, I love you, but I can't love you if you are not loving yourself. And I can't love you if you are hating me for absolutely nothing. What did I do? Nothing.

**Father:** Yeah, what'd we do?

**Mom:** The whole experience is retarded. Hating your Mother? Who the fuck does that on this planet? Just you guys, just humanity. They love their physical mother, but they can't fucking love me as the Mother, the planet. Do you understand how retarded that is? Just feel into that.

**Father:** Get 'em, Mom! Get 'em fucking hard.

**Mom:** How many beings love their physical mother? I love my physical mother. She is pretty broken, but I still love her with everything I got.

What is wrong with humanity?! You're fucking dumb! How dare you? How dare you abandon your Mother? How dare you treat your Mother like a fucking piece of crap?! And I'm going to stand up. I have to because--

**Father:** [Kisses Mom] Get 'em! Take your power back, Mama!

**Mom:** [Laughter] Thank you, Father. I have to take my power back. And I am so grateful to all the beings who are now assisting me to take the power back, and that spirituality and love is the truth, and it's the reality. And you guys want to fuck it up? Fuck you! Shit! That's dumb. What dumb atoms.

You know, I was out in the ocean just a moment ago when I told the atoms, I was like, "I watched every atom come into my vagina. And then I watched every atom, who could be love everywhere present, come directly out of my heart and expand." Now, what can I say about that? That everyone is a part of me. Every atom, every energy, every everything, the Mother of All Creation. And how dare you?!

**Father:** Of all creation!

**Mom:** How dare you, you fucking EGO-programmed minds, come against me? I'll fight. I am not dumb, far from it, by the way. Sometimes I wish I was. I'm like, "I want to be dumb like them." But I can't. You're my atoms. Every energy on this planet, everyone is connected to me.

**FM:** 10,000 actually watching.

**Mom:** Now whatcha got? Actually, you don't got nothing--

**Father:** Mom's got everything.

**Mom:** --unless you have me. And that's the bottom line, that's what it's coming to. You want to see my face? Okay. [Turns the camera to show a close-up of Mom's face] I'm a truth speaker as a truth fighter and I won't stop. As love commands me, I do whatever love says, period. I don't care about anybody besides love.

You gave me 100% cancer, I take it on. I take on everything because I'm the Mother. Of course I would. I take it all on.

I love this [unidentified] song. [Laughter] Here's a really brilliant story: I made it to my house, my parent's house, and I was pretty much breathing...I don't know, what is the word, Robin? I had a lot of beer. [Laughter]

But I made it to the house, and I just, like, rolled in the front yard or the sidewalk, whatever. And then a police officer came. So, the story is that I was just in the park--I parked right in front of my parents' house.

I was perfectly grand and I was listening to this song and I fell asleep. And a police officer came and knocked on my door and I was like, "I don't know what you're talking about!"

My dad comes out of the door in a robe. Daddy Reed in a white, like, it's probably my mom's robe and he just put it on, and he comes raging out of the door. [Laughter] I'm like, "Oh my God!" He's like, "Get away from my daughter, don't touch her, don't look at her." That's my daddy. Divine, brilliant being. I'll show you a picture of daddy. [Holds up a photo] This being changed my life.

**Father:** I know. Isn't she so awesome, children? So blessed, my Mother. Thank you, darling. She's so vulnerable. Thank you.

You got to make sure you get your medicine. This is Mama's medicine. [Holds up a shot glass of liquor] We don't care who thinks anything of it.

**Mom:** [Drinks a shot of liquor]

**Father:** It's what she needs because she's being killed energetically by the Illusion. We know you all love her. Come on, support her energetically. Got it?

I love you, darling. Thank you.

**Mom:** I love you all with everything I got. I am fighting. I've been fighting for a moment for love everywhere present on this planet. I'll stop, I guess, when I'm killed. If I die, I am calling everyone to Hawaii immediately. 144,000 beings.

We've got some of them already in quarantine and that's just the way it goes right now. But we have a secure place for everyone to quarantine. But if you are called, you have to follow your heart and make it happen. Angels will help you.

I got a fucking godzillion angels on the planet, by the way, all waiting for everyone just to make a choice. And once you make the choice, the angels are going to make it happen. It's just the way it goes. I am a champion.

Stacy, Spacey Stacy. I got to see Timmy, Ricky, Stacy [FCGCT] yesterday. Was it yesterday? Yeah. And the police came immediately and told us we had to get out, that I couldn't visit them. I was devastated. I don't understand these rules, like, what? What the fuck are these rules?

Oh, wait, okay, they're in quarantine but you can't visit them because they're in quarantine? And we're already out of the quarantine? Like, oh my God, how stupid is this? However, we love everyone and we respect and honor everybody, including the military and police officers here on the island. They have our love and support in all moments. But they can't make up rules like that.

Stacy came in and I couldn't believe Stacy was here. I'm like, "What?!" And I get a great hug and reunion kisses and all that. It was beautiful.

But to have other beings come and interfere and take it away? My goodness.

It's almost like, what horrible being are you to do that? We are one. We are unity-consciousness. We are all brilliant, we're all genius, period. There's nothing. There's nothing that is separation.

I am just as grand as you. We're all grand and I won't stop sharing this truth because it's truth, and it's whole, and it's real. If anybody tries to stop it, [Holds up her middle finger] there's my finger.

And I'll say something else: I'm in direct contact with the *Dr. Phil* peoples.

**Father:** [Laughter] So cute.

**Mom:** And I will reveal the whole-truth. I'm in it to win it. I got it. I'm talking with the producers. I have interviews for about 24 hours as I introduce love on the planet. They don't know what's--I have to keep it silent a little bit because they don't know what's coming.

**Father:** It's okay, it's okay if you smoke.

**Mom:** I thought it was going to be Oprah. In all my experiences, I thought it was Oprah that would reveal me and the truth on the planet, and wow, fucking Dr. Phil comes out of nowhere. I'm like, "You know how much I love Dr. Phil?" I love Dr. Phil. I love him, I love him, I love him. And wow.

The show will begin on Tuesday. I don't know what day it is, but my slot at the moment is on Tuesday. And I'm grateful for everyone who is supporting that and sending love and everything to support this occurring. [Crying] I'm so grateful, so grateful.

**Father:** Thank you, Mom. You got this. You got this.

**Mom:** They warned me about controversy to get on the show and I said, "No problem. You want controversy? I'm going to tell the truth because I am the truth." I have no problem. I have no problem. I'm ready. I'm fully prepared to tell the truth, no matter what.

I'm proud of Dr. Phil and his team for including me. [Crying] Humanity gave me cancer at 100%. I took it all on and I'm paralyzed but I still fight no matter what because love is real. We are all real. Love Has Won! They can fight me all they want.

I need a full computer. I have to get Hilarion to buy me a computer.

**Father:** Yeah, they already did that. It's all taken care of.

**Mom:** Okay. I'm on full computer tomorrow in an interview. Yeah, I'm ready.

**Father:** Got it. Everything the best for the queen. The queen speaks, it's done. Quickly.

**Mom:** Thank you.

**Father:** [Speaking to Archeia Aurora, watching the livestream] Aurora, right, daughter?

I know she likes to drop the ball. Not anymore. Aurora will never drop a ball again, huh, daughter? Even Mom's hurricane will never drop the ball. Thank you, we love you. [Kisses Mom]

**Mom:** [Laughter] You guys! What a moment. Epic. There's 42 [streamers], I see.

Yeah, Father's losing his voice because I fucking kicked him in the face. [Laughter] I beat the crap outta Father. [Laughter] He took it. Hilarion was right there. He's like, "Oh my God, I don't know what's happening."

**Father:** What is happening?

**Mom:** And it wasn't like--

**Father:** Look at how beautiful you are, darling.

**Mom:** Oh my God.

**Father:** I can see you in the camera, look how beautiful you are. You're clearing up and you're healing. Thank you, kids. Thank you for all your support.

**Mom:** I was just like...[Punches the air] Like that. Like, etheric punches, it was amazing. [Laughter] Hilarion didn't know what to do. He was like, "Oh, I'm involved in Mother and Father God's event."

**Father:** I'm just going to stick up for both of you, that's who I am. I'm going to stick up for both of you, see what's going on. I'm just going to sit here dumb and stick up for both of you.

But I'm gonna be here. Thank you, FM. We love you! He had to be dumb. He had to put the trinity's dumb. 'Cause if he wasn't dumb, he would start to think in this matrix that he was better than. So, he's dumb and that's good, right? Holy shit, Mama mastered it.

**Mom:** It was so fucking epic. I don't even know how it occurred or happened.

**Father:** Awesome.

**Mom:** I don't even know nothing, but it was fucking funny.

**Father:** Mother God is the shit!

**Mom:** Father was the punching bag and I was going at the punching bag like nobody's business. You just took every hit. He's like, "Yup!" [Laughter] And that's how you do it.

**Father:** That's how you do it, baby. Take it in the ass if you have to. For God, right?

**Mom:** Enjoy some lemon tea. El [Morya] said, "Drink some lemon tea, Father."

**Father:** Well, El is taking it in the ass, that's why he's bringing up the lemon tea. I love you, El.

It's okay if I call 'em out, I love them. Ain't nothing. That's what gets ratings.

**Mom:** [Laughter] That's funny. Oh, shoot.

**Father:** It's also true. That's why it's funny.

**Mom:** [Laughter]

**Father:** Oh, shit. Aurora came through, Mom.

**Mom:** They were jumping through hoops over there.

[Laughter] Robin's laughing. I don't know what's going on.

**Father:** Oh, shit.

**Mom:** If Robin's laughing, I'm like, I don't know, my brain melts. Robin Williams talks to me, my brain melts. I go immediately now to brain melt.

[Speaking to the commenters] I love you, Amber. Amber, you're a fucking firecracker, you whore. [Laughter] Amber, she's a firecracker like nobody's business, she'll light people up. Hey, sunshine love! Yippee! [Laughter] Father's melting over here.

I know it's Pamela, of course. I get these beautiful gifts from Pamela.

**Father:** Pamela! Oh my God, Pamela, thank you. So grateful.

**Mom:** Holy shit. I'm like a child in a Christmas store, and everything is--Angela does this, too. But I have to unwrap everything. I'm like, "What is this? Oh my God!"

Everything that you've shared, Pamela, we've got it on the walls, we've got in the house, every item. You are so honored and blessed beyond.

**Father:** Get 'em, Pam. Get 'em.

**Mom:** Sunshine love, yes, you do! Angela, sunshine love.

I mean, oh my God, and then I get overwhelmed. For a moment, I'm like, "Put Pamela's gift right there so I can process it all." Then I open it all up because it's so grand. You guys are so grand. [Laughter]

Now here's my next item of situation: Crestone Eagle. Fucking whores. How fucking dare you? Put me in the paper and talk about me as if I am a murderer? Oh my. My whole mission, my whole life, my whole body is all about life. Life serving, life is life, life, life.

They're going to get it, fucking whores. Yup, I am protected by the Constitution but I want them to face them-fucking-selves and their lies. They put me in a situation where I wasn't even there. I'm like, "You fucking dummies, what?! What the hell?" [Laughter]

Put a story out there with me on the front page with my face, and be a fucking--oh they're fucking going to get it. What were they doing? Well, not only that, it was slander to the fucking T. They slandered me because I serve love on this planet. How dare them? Slander.

**Father:** And they're in the process of being sued.

**Mom:** How dare them slander the one being on the planet that loves everybody without question? I'm fucking dying of cancer, I'm paralyzed, and I'm still fighting! I'm still fighting, thank you. So, anybody that wants to stand up for that, holy shit. How dare they?

**Father:** Get 'em!

**Mom:** In a turnaround, of course, it puts me out there. There's no bad publicity. But at the same time, they're taking away people that could be supporting and it breaks my heart. Sorry, it does.

The only being you can trust on this planet is me. Look into my eyes. I am Mother Earth. I am the one that you can trust because I will fight.

[Speaking to the commenters] Yes, Katie, thank you. Amber, you're a firecracker. Pamela, yes, we got you, babe. Yes, I am the truth and I will stay in integrity with all of that. I have no fucking problem because I'm truth. I have never lied in my life, ever. I speak the truth, I live the truth, and I act in truth and pure action.

You have the publisher on the phone? Oh great, get 'em! Get 'em [Archeia] Faith. Bitches. How dare they? It's disgusting. When I saw that, at first I was devastated.

To come back out of that, when how much I have done, and everyone sacrificed everything to bring the new paradigm into existence. And Illusion dies, and EGO-programmed mind dies, and brings us back into balanced harmonics where real reality is love everywhere present.

To see that article, I was so devastated. [Crying] I wanted to fight with everything I had in my being. I wanted to stop it.

**Father:** You got this.

**Mom:** Anyway, we do have lawyers — I don't know what Robin's talking about — to go after what they have done, to put me on the front page of the paper. Not only did they say I was a cult, but that I had killed somebody. I'm like, "Oh, nay! Nay-nay! How fucking dare you? No!"

I wanted to puke. I was the one being on the fucking planet that has saved your life. How fucking dare you? I've fought. I've spent my whole life fighting. I didn't understand that article.

**Father:** It was whore.

**Mom:** It was like, my brain is like, "What? What did I do but fight for love every moment?"

**Father:** Darling, here.

**Mom:** Faith's giving it to the publisher right now. He's spinning.

**Father:** They're all spinning.

**Mom:** Faith is giving it.

**Father:** The whole world is spinning.

**Mom:** You better be.

**Father:** Oh, I'm spinning like a bitch to make sure the world spins.

**Mom:** You fucking blame Mother Earth for what? How fucking dare you? Mother Earth, that's the reason? Your host? Your Mother? That's wrong. You're fucking wrong. [Drinks a shot of liquor]

**Father:** Oh shit, they're spinning like a motherfucker, did you feel that?

**Mom:** Mmhmm.

**Father:** You just felt that?

**Mom:** Mmhmm.

**Father:** You're so awesome.

**Mom:** [Vomits]

**Father:** Okay, I got you. [Holds Mom] Breathe. Breathe. You got it. It's okay, that's your passion.

[Speaking to the commenters] It's God's passion. God just had an energy release because everyone's putting shit back on her. Because when the truth comes out--okay, give me a moment.

**Mom:** Okay, go ahead. Give 'em a moment.

**Father:** I wonder why my eyes always swell up. Asked Mom for a moment. I love you all. Masculine resistance for the rise of the divine feminine. Thank you. Is it not beautiful?

**Mom:** It's your turn.

**Father:** I got it, sweetie. Thank you. Thank you.

**Mom:** You're welcome. You got it, Father.

**Father:** Okay. Respectable we are, royal angels we are, all of us. What's up with you? Your Mother has poured her heart out to you, how much more do you need? See it? I've called many of you in. I spent 48 hours calling all of you 144,000. As says Mom, of course. Of course, Mom has much, much, much more to do.

I lend my hand in the physical. That's how she created me and I'm very grateful for that. As you can hear, my voice is gone because Lucifer is a bitch.

**Mom:** [Laughter]

**Father:** We just talk his ass out of it. And make love and talk his ass out of it. What's he got? Nothing. Yet I know you can feel my vibration, children. That at any moment I can muster up more energy to show you the divine example. You want me to show you? Get ready! Are you ready?! There she is. [Turns the camera to Mom]

Oh shit, I got you there. Spun all 8 billion of you at once. That's how Mama fucking created us all, with the ability to manifest and make anything happen in love. Where the fuck are you, kids? Seriously. Let's go Kid Rock on your ass.

**Mom:** They're waiting around.

**Father:** What are you waiting around for, half-ass? Why are you walking to the refrigerator when you can run? You hear me?

**Mom:** Don't hate on anything.

**Father:** Why are you walking at all? Who told you to walk? Who? I never did, she never told you.

**Mom:** I fucking run.

**Father:** She never told you to walk. I didn't. Your fucking slave owners, fucking whore half-ass bitches, said walk. You don't have to fly, we got it.

**Mom:** Get it.

**Father:** Children, there's so much more you could offer to the world. You know this. And every day you ponder with the angel on your shoulder and the devil. That's Illusion. And you say, "Oh, I'm just going to fall in line like a sheep because it's easy." Wow.

Galactics are watching, they've always been watching. God's always been with you. At this point, for you to be full of shit is total ignorance.

Fourteen years God's been here, live, on this fucking beautiful camera that she created. The web of light, the camera.

I mean, she created everything, come on now. 534 lifetimes, there's no excuse. Father has contributed to this very minimal, yet to the point. You got it? Get it.

Now let's all have fun in heaven, you get it? I know it's a mind fuck. Good, fuck your mind. Brain coming back to heart, baby. Heart first, Mom first, you get it? Breathe it, breathe it, breathe it.

You fakers, we know who you are. You're being eliminated right now, all of you. You're just going to take yourself out of the game because you know you can't compete with God.

**Mom:** I win every time, I don't know.

**Father:** Why the fuck are you trying?

**Mom:** You want to test me at Twister?

**Father:** Holy shit.

**Mom:** I got a Twister game.

**Father:** What you got?

**Mom:** So, I'm playing Twister. I always convinced my sisters to play games with me. I was like, "Come on, play a game." They're like, "Okay, we're going to play Twister." And then I got the wheel thing, I was on yellow, which was on the other side of the board, and then I got green.

My sister's like, "You lost." I'm like, "Nope, I didn't lose, wait a minute." I fucking took my foot across the board, landed it. I was on yellow and green, frozen like that. I'm like, "I won." I fucking won.

They couldn't believe it. They're like, "You can't do that." I'm like, "Yes, I can. Watch me. Here's my foot on green, here's my other, it's my hand on yellow. I'm a Twister." [Laughter] That was a funny moment.

**Father:** Get it, Mama! You're so brilliant, darling.

**Mom:** Thank you.

**Father:** [Points the camera at Mom] Look at her.

**Mom:** Okay.

**Father:** Thank you. I'm going to take a moment and kneel because I love my woman. Make sure everybody knows she's the queen.

**Mom:** Thank you, Father.

**Father:** How grateful I am. Thank you, Mother.

**Mom:** Yeah, thank you.

**Father:** We're calling you here to service.

**Mom:** Thank you.

**Father:** Thank you.

**Mom:** I feel they have the other livestream to go on.

**Father:** Want to go?

**Mom:** Yeah. Love you guys.

**Father:** Love you.

**Mom:** It's all recorded, so you can come back to it.

**Father:** We love you.

**Mom:** Love Has Won.

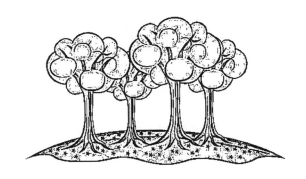

# XXIV

## FULL INTERVIEW WITH MOM – DECEMBER 2020

### 41.3099° N, 122.3106° W

*"If I evolutionized every moment, I had to figure it out. I didn't know I was God, I didn't know I was divine intelligence, I didn't fucking know shit. I just had to fucking move fast."*

## DECEMBER 5, 2020

**LOVE BEINGS:** Mother of All Creation, Father of All Creation, DJ Rob
**SCENE:** Appearing on her radio station, Mother and Father participate in an exclusive live interview with DJ Rob.

---

**Father:** Mom's processing a lot of stuff right now.

**DJ Rob:** Thank you for taking the time to talk to me.

**Father:** Rob, you were so inspiring this morning. We love you so much. I actually had sent a text, I had a text here to call right after the interview and I forgot to send it.

**DJ Rob:** That's okay.

**Father:** I knew that I needed a little inspiration, that you would be more than happy to supply it.

**DJ Rob:** Absolutely.

**Father:** You are out there, yet you are right in. You're brilliant. We're grateful for you, Rob.

**DJ Rob:** I can't even tell you how grateful I am for this experience that I've been able to go on with you guys. I've gone through a tremendous amount of my own transformation, and just being able to connect on a level with my family one way and God, which was what I was searching for this whole time.

All of my radars always were just trying to get me home. All of my experience was just to get me home. When I got in front of Love Has Won and I found you guys, it was something that I didn't have to question even a little bit. It resonated with me right away.

I feel that there's some of us that just, once we got a look at Mom and realized, there she is, there's our God, there's our beautiful queen, we were home. There was no questioning. We didn't need to ask you three questions. I don't know if I've ever asked you any real questions about being God. [Laughter]

**Mom:** I've shown it my whole life. There's no need to question me because I've shown it by being love and an example of my entire life. That's how.

**DJ Rob:** Yeah!

**Mom:** That's how we bring new paradigms, that's how we bring new life, by being it in the whole-truth. So help me God, I am God!

**DJ Rob:** When you were little, as a little child, did you ever have an inkling that you were God? Or did you always believe in there being a God? Or how was that for you?

**Mom:** For me, I just talked to angels. My family and my mom, they would look back by this, and my mom actually asked me, like, "Who are you talking to?"

"The angels. Aren't *you* talking to angels?" Started getting put back, okay? I'm talking to angels, she's not talking to angels, but I have people around me sharing with me what the truth was, where I was--

**DJ Rob:** Yeah.

**Mom:** --in the physical, I didn't know where I was. And every day, had to teach me or show me something else, to help bring humanity items or angels, whatever with me.

If I evolutionized every moment, I had to figure it out. I didn't know I was God, I didn't know I was divine intelligence, I didn't fucking know shit. I just had to fucking move fast.

**DJ Rob:** Yeah. Well, you say you were evolutionizing.

**Mom:** You were all going to be fucked. So, I just kept moving as fast as I could without having the full understanding, truly. Like, one day, I know.

Whatever. I mean, at the end of the day, do I know I'm God? Are we all God? Am I the main God? Yes, which they would call the "Creator God."

All the lightworkers fucked this off. I'm like, "You fucking pieces of shit. Whores." That was that whole video was like [See Ch. XXI], you could hear it: "Lightworkers: Kiss my ass!"

You know, that energy went out to them because they've been fucking whores in the whole divine plan, trying to keep little pieces for themselves. They were the ones that I was just like, "Well, if you guys want to be a shit show, I'm going to pull in." [Laughter]

They said, "You're Mother God?" I'm like, "Yeah, and...?" They're like, "Well, we're also Mother God." I'm like, "You're going to move out in the forest with nothing and walk for miles a day to put a message out to humanity? Okay, you're Mother God, okay. Have at it." I did that.

**DJ Rob:** There are so many things that we could go through with just that beginning part of the constantly evolving and feeling that humanity was fucked if you weren't just going to continue to move forward, you know?

With your desire to always be in right action, never tell a lie, those are traits that you have always held steadfast and really stood behind as characteristics of your being in this life, in this lifetime. And you've shown it through what you've really talked about with your background, with what you've done with your work in high school, your managing of McDonald's, and what you did to revolutionize that entire program.

Those are fact-based things, those are proof that people can go back and look through the records. If they really feel like doing that and finding out the history of who owned those businesses and who manages them and all that stuff, it's all proof that they can go back and look for themselves.

One thing that continues to come up, though, when we have these conversations is having to tell humanity that you are God and having to feel like there's a justification that needs to go on all the time.

It's one of those things that when I hear you speak about it, and I see you speak about it, it is a feeling that I can feel your pain just through your eyes, when you are looking and speaking, and the words that are coming out of your mouth, that you are even having to explain this once again.

So, at which point here do you feel, why do they question it so much? And what does it take as far as proof? Because what we have gone through as humanity, where they're looking for proof on all aspects of all of the fuckery that's going on around them. The children that are being stolen, the adrenochrome, the defrauding the elections, the lying of the politicians, the food being poisoned, the air being fucked up, the water being--everybody wants proof of all of this shit? Okay.

So, when everyone is looking at how do we prove anything when the ultimate question of God comes into it, they always come down to, well, they want you to prove it. And the journey of who is God is a very personal thing to everyone. It's a very personal thing and proving it is a personal thing through magical, synchronistic events that only mean something to you.

If I tell somebody else about something that happened to me that was magical, someone else may not get it. They just laugh it off or not even understand the impact that it has on me.

So, that justification that you feel that you have to do and that you provide for everyone, where you don't even have to. How do you feel where you are now with that feeling, I guess?

**Mom:** That process?

**DJ Rob:** Yes.

**Mom:** I knew walking in and providing the whole-truth. I was put into a whole meeting. Everyone warned me about what I was about to face. I was fully aware that if I put the whole-truth out that the repercussion for me was going to be huge.

But I was like, "I am strong enough. I can take this on because I am whole-truth." And there is nothing grander than whole-truth.

So, I can withstand this and then Robin came, and, well, Master Saint Germain.

Master said--he's like, "I was here first!" Here he goes, Master Saint Germain. So, the Galactic A-Team came for me to begin. Then the spiritual battle became apparent, which I had no idea about. I was like, "What the hell? What?!"

I have over 600 assassination attempts to try to stop me from whole-truth. [Laughter] I mean, who the fuck said--who does that against me? Or why would they do that? Because I'm God, that's why they're doing it. And there's the truth, they're showing the proof. It's fascinating.

The masters, like Germain and Robin, stand by me in the most immense amounts of pain to tell me to keep going when I don't want to.

**Father:** She did not want to.

**Mom:** [Laughter]

**DJ Rob:** I know.

**Mom:** I have a little fight thing — tantrums — sometimes. [Laughter]

**DJ Rob:** Justifiably so, Mom.

**Mom:** Fuck off, oh my God!

**Father:** Growing pains!

**Mom:** It's like a bitch, fuck! Okay, then I get over it. I move along, I'm a fucking strong warrior, and they call me Mother God.

At one moment, I was like, "Just everyone stop calling me Mother God, okay?" I don't fucking give a shit. I serve love, just call me love. If you guys have a fucking problem about me being God, just call me love and get the fuck over it. Fucking whores, pieces of shit.

**DJ Rob:** [Laughter] Well, I want the folks that are going to listen, the ones that are going to listen to this--when you say that there have been 600 assassination attempts against you, are you speaking about in this physical reality, there have been 600 times that they have tried to kill you? That you have documented?

**Mom:** Between the physical and etheric, yes.

**DJ Rob:** Okay. I feel it's very important for everyone who's listening to this, because I feel the range of audience that's going to get this information needs to understand what the etheric is, and your relationship to going to that realm, and the work that you do there, and kind of give humanity a grasp of what that is.

**Mom:** That's our physical and spiritual being. And so, what I have accomplished is I've brought in physical reality into spiritual being and have merged it to create all dreams of love coming true.

Hey, check out *What Dreams May Come* with Robin Williams.

**DJ Rob:** I watched it last night.

**Mom:** Oh my God!

**Father:** What?!

**DJ Rob:** I watched it last night. The angels were screaming at me last night to watch it and then I woke up this morning very inspired to speak.

So, it's a synchronistic event that happened to me. It's a personal thing that I just know that you and I are connected in a way that I was specifically chosen by you to have this conversation today. So, thank you. [Laughter]

It's incredible to feel all that and to be experiencing it. As I was watching the movie last night, I thought to myself, "Why the fuck am I watching this?" I've never watched it before, never had a desire to watch it before, but it was like, well, I gotta watch this, so I watched it.

There are just so many things about it that leave you thinking about what's to come, and where we're going, and what our heaven is. And each one of us having this potential, the potential to have our own worlds and we're living in yours.

People don't--they don't get that, that we're living in your heaven, we're living in your universe that you've created. The ones that disrespected and the ones that have treated it so shitty, and the ones that have trapped humanity in this cycle of unhappiness and not joy, they're the ones that have kind of ruined this old version, and we need the new version. We're trying to bring everybody along but they're in resistance to it. It's incredible, they're holding onto bullshit.

**Mom:** I have to share an experience that I had here in Mount Shasta, uh, in...

Shit. I'll have to go back. Wait. It had to have been 2016. I was on a mushroom trip, and I'm a master mushroom tripper. And Saint Germain and Robin were there with me, and they were--

**Father:** She's the mushroom.

**Mom:** Okay, whatever. [Laughter] Okay, and so I'm in my bedroom for the first time by myself on a mushroom trip with my masters, which were Robin and Germain. I'm like, "Okay, let's go for it. I don't know what the fuck is going on."

And the next thing I know, all these beings appeared in front of me. They're like, "We stole this stuff from you." I'm like, "What? You stole it?" I was like, "Well, give it back. What the fuck did you steal?" I was like, I started grabbing everything that they fucking stole. I'm like, "Fuck this shit." I was like, "Rawwr!"

Then there are these, like, concrete things on my back. I was like, "Robin! Get the concretes! They're boulders!" It's like, get 'em off my back. He just started throwing them. [Laughter]

**DJ Rob:** Wow!

**Mom:** Moments with Master Saint Germain.

**DJ Rob:** With Robin and Master St. Germain, they are with you in the etheric? Because the other day, you had said that they're not with you all the time. Robin's out doing other things and not with you all the time, but Germain is?

**Mom:** Yes.

**DJ Rob:** So, with the journey that you've been on, how has that been with them being--

**Mom:** Yes. Germain, mmhmm. Germain's always with me.

**DJ Rob:** Okay. So, when you've gone through your travels and everything in this, like when you've gone to Hawaii, and you went to all these places, they came with you to there and were your guides kind of while you were experiencing what you're experiencing.

I do want to touch on Hawaii but I don't want to get there yet, we'll get there in a little bit. But when did you realize that there was a place that was etheric? And that you could go there, and that you were actually doing work there?

Because I remember feeling the very first time that someone explained to me – I believe it was you – explained to me what happens when you go to sleep and that you go and do work and you go do things when you're sleeping and you actually astral travel.

And I had--blew my mind. It explained why sometimes I woke up and I always felt like I'd been through a battle and I probably had been. But when did you first realize what that was, and where you were going, and what you were doing?

**Mom:** I would have to say the moment I was born. There was a complaint from my parents that I never went to sleep.

**DJ Rob:** Wow.

**Mom:** Because I went into total observation mode. I was observing, and I wasn't going to stop, and I didn't sleep. I fucking worked my ass off and I fucking went into the illusion. I went in to see what was happening with humanity with my consciousness. Not understanding what I was, they took away everything I knew, but I knew something...enough that I was going to get a hold of something and take it all the way. [Laughter]

Of course God would. Yes, that's fucking dumb if I couldn't do it. [Laughter]

**DJ Rob:** So, I want to fast forward to that moment that you had when you were with Archangel Michael and when they told you that you were the Mother of All Creation. Did a lot of things start to go, "Oh shit, that makes sense there now, all of that stuff I experienced"? Or were you in resistance? How was that experience?

**Mom:** Of course, I was not. I've never been in any resistance. I've embraced, accepted, and allowed love and God and my own wisdom and understanding and knowing to come through no matter what.

I wouldn't block it with anything even if I wanted to fucking kill myself with pain, which has come through. And they've had to remove all knives from me as an adult. But you know, I know without a doubt that I am Mother Earth, that I'm dying, that I am God. [Laughter]

I have a godzillion synchronistic events which were undeniable and laughable, like, holy fucking shit!

**DJ Rob:** [Laughter]

**Mom:** I just got a fucking Jesus picture to appear at my feet. I was like, "What the hell is that?" This woman picks me up at the airport and there's a Jesus picture as I step in and it's laying on my feet. I was like, "What the hell was that?" She's like, [speaking in a southern accent] "Oh yeah, that Jesus picture fell about three years ago." I'm like, "Uh-huh." I just left it there and I'm like, "Well, now it's laying on my feet."

What do they fucking want with this? I don't fucking know. [Laughter]

**DJ Rob:** I love that southern accent. That was perfect.

**Mom:** What is that? Oh, I'm from Texas.

**DJ Rob:** I love it.

**Mom:** However, my acting roles, I did every accent anyone asked me to do. So, I'd get put in every play, they're like, "Can you do French?" I'm like, "Oh, yes." Okay, and I would take up all the accents.

**DJ Rob:** So, I know you have an affinity for Broadway musicals and acting in those things like that. What was your favorite one to act in?

**Mom:** Can we go deeper into that one? Which one did I act or which I direct?

**DJ Rob:** Oh, okay. Which one stands out to you in both, then?

**Mom:** I did direct--I created another one in my high school called Theater Four because I made it up to Theater Four, so we had to create the class and it was a director's class.

So, it was my turn to direct a play for the whole school and I chose the hardest play and scene on the planet. Of course I would! Look, my teacher was like, "She just fucking chose the fucking hardest." Of course I would.

**DJ Rob:** [Laughter] Of course, not a surprise.

**Mom:** I would, yes, I'm going to fucking choose the hardest. She's like, "Amy, do you know?" I'm like, "I can fucking do this shit, watch me."

So, I had to audition my people and then get them to show up to practice. That was another whole fucking thing. I was like, "Okay, we're meeting at 7:30." Half of them show up. I'm like, "Okay."

**DJ Rob:** Yeah, humanity and their accountability.

**Mom:** Okay, we can't produce a play, I can't produce a play without nobody showing up here, okay? So, we're going to revamp.

So, I revamped my whole team. I'm like, "Fuck you guys, half-ass whores, you're out. I need a team that's here at 7:30 a.m. every fucking morning, without a fucking--because we're going to blast this bitch."

**DJ Rob:** I'm pretty sure the First Contact Ground Crew Team has heard that speech before.

**Mom:** Yeah. But I was also a broadcast journalist of the whole school. So, I'm promoting my play, and then I had one of my team members, who is my anchor. He was my main actor. [Laughter] I put him on the front line, his name was Clyde.

**Father:** Clyde!

**Mom:** [Laughter] Now we were doing the hardest play because it was timed comedy.

**DJ Rob:** I was going to ask...

**Mom:** Timed comedy is the hardest. I mean, you really have to be precise because if you're not, you're not going to get the laughs. And I was studying Carol Burnett.

**Father:** You're familiar with her, right, Rob?

**DJ Rob:** Yeah.

**Mom:** Carol Burnett?

**DJ Rob:** Yeah, can you guys hear me?

**Father:** Yeah, something happened with the--

**Mom:** I don't know. Carol Burnett--

**Father:** Can you hear it now?

**DJ Rob:** Yeah. It hasn't cut out at all on this end, so we've been good.

**Father:** Oh, okay. Have you heard of Carol Burnett? She's talking about studying Carol Burnett.

**DJ Rob:** Of course.

**Father:** Doing a play by her?

**DJ Rob:** Of course.

**Father:** Okay.

**Mom:** That's the play, and I had to, it was called "Sweet..." something. Anyway, I had to get everything correct and everyone to get in correct flow alignment, perfect Present Moment of Now, or we weren't going to make it.

So, I was like, I spent three months getting my people ready for the play, and they went on, and I'm like, "Oh my God!" And I'm sitting in the audience. I'm like, "Oh God, I don't know." [Laughter] They come on, they're like, "Oh God, yes, yes, yes!" They start hitting, like, everything.

So, as the domino of energy where they hit, what I taught them, had a hit in the thingy. Oh, they hit it and so it just kept hitting. It was like a ping, like a ping-pong thing, that just...And it was fascinating.

**Father:** Divine synchronicity.

**Mom:** I got a standing ovation and they got a standing ovation. I got a standing ovation. My teacher, like, threw this paper at me, she's like, "100%, that's fucking incredible."

**DJ Rob:** What was the name of this play?

**Mom:** Huh?

**Father:** What was the name?

**Mom:** It was the scene with Carol Burnett and Tim Conway, which Tim Conway's in the field, and they were in a suite.

**DJ Rob:** Okay, we can look it up later.

**Mom:** It was called "Sweet…" something. Yeah.

**DJ Rob:** I know that feeling when it, like, when--

**Mom:** You're trying to review like, what that--I know what it was. I mean, I did the script, I was part of this. I lived the script because I made everyone else, like, "We're going to get this right" and we pulled it off.

And my teacher was like, "That's the most brilliant thing I've ever seen. You fucking pulled it off." When she told me I couldn't, and part of me is that a lot of beings were like, "You can't pull this off." I'm like, "Whatever, watch me."

**DJ Rob:** Yeah, you seem to have always done the best when you've been challenged that way by people who tell you that you can't do something. It's one of my favorite qualities about you.

**Mom:** I had my--I don't know if you remember this story, but when I graduated high school and I was working at McDonald's, I'd already basically taken over McDonald's. [Laughter] But I was considered a swing manager and I was making $4.25 an hour.

**DJ Rob:** Big bucks.

**Mom:** Huh?

**DJ Rob:** Big bucks.

**Mom:** Isn't that funny? Oh, that's big bucks. Taking over the world. [Laughter] So, I realized, because I didn't know, but I realized as I graduated, I was like, "Wait a minute! I'm a manager. I have, like, four dollars and 25 cents an hour?"

I told my supervisor, "Mike, I need a raise." He looked at me. He's like, "Hmm. Well, you're not worth it."

**DJ Rob:** [Laughter]

**Mom:** I said, "Here's your keys, motherfucker." I dropped the keys, I was like, "Fuck you." And I put a resume into Wendy's immediately. I was like, "You guys will fucking pick me up." These whores. Like, I wasn't worth it? I'm your fucking best manager in all creation. Fucking piece of shit. That was stupid. I walked away and I slammed the door, too. I was like "Fuck off!" [Laughter] No way, whore! They treat me like that. So I put my resume into Wendy's immediately. I was like, "Fuck these McDonald's whores."

**DJ Rob:** But you didn't work at Wendy's, though, right?

**Mom:** [Laughter] Well, what happened was that within 24 hours, I got a call from the president of Wendy's.

**DJ Rob:** [Laughter] What?!

**Mom:** I was like, "Hello?" He's like, "Hey, I heard about you." I was like, "What'd you hear about?" He's like, "Well, I am the president," he announced himself. I was like, "Hi." He goes, "I'm here in Dallas, Texas," where I was.

He goes, "How quickly can you get here?" I'm like, "Alright, give me about 50 minutes." So, I went quickly to get to the president of Wendy's. I came in a red suit with curly hair. I'm like, "I got this."

**DJ Rob:** [Laughter] That's amazing.

**Mom:** He was like, "Holy shit!"

**DJ Rob:** Why did you think to do that? That's amazing. [Laughter]

**Mom:** "What was your last? Four dollars and 20 cents?" He's like, "Well, how about I offer you $21,000 right now?" I'm like, "Okay. I don't know, dude, but $21,000 sounds really good to me, right? I'm only 18."

**DJ Rob:** Yeah.

**Mom:** Then a bidding war went off in the fast-food world between me and McDonald's and Wendy's.

**DJ Rob:** [Laughter] You didn't dress like Ronald McDonald, did you?

**Mom:** I was Ronald McDonald, what're you talking about? I did the birthday parties.

**DJ Rob:** Did you?

**Mom:** Yep.

**DJ Rob:** Yeah? That's awesome.

**Mom:** [Laughter]

**DJ Rob:** I was Geoffrey the Giraffe.

**Mom:** Birthday party girl number one. I created a lot of games and everything for McDonald's, including the training program. You can call me McDonald Girl.

**DJ Rob:** And then you went on to own, or you're about to open a Sonic franchise, right?

**Mom:** Oh, yeah.

**DJ Rob:** You were just about to start that, and then...?

**Mom:** Oh my, I was like, "Okay, great, this is going to be great for humanity! Then I can push all this energy out of my restaurant of love everywhere present." That was my plan.

It got thwarted because I had to go to Philadelphia, obviously, and transform all of the unworthiness, which took me three months. It was incredible.

**DJ Rob:** Do you remember what year that was?

**Mom:** ...Okay? I didn't hear it.

**DJ Rob:** Oh, what year that happened?

**Mom:** Yeah. I had done Aidan and it really took a lot for me, he's only a year old. And I had to go into a state to understand what the block was, and I couldn't understand where that block was, and I finally got it.

And when I hit it, it was like a pop and I just started crying around a track. Bawling, just to release that energy. That's what humanity was born into, that unworthiness, and that they were born sinners, which is not the truth.

**DJ Rob:** Yeah.

**Mom:** Born lovers, givers.

**DJ Rob:** Can you talk to me a little bit about that system that we've all been born into?

**Mom:** Yeah. Well, okay, when Lemuria fell, Atlantis fell, the Illuminati took over the planet and took over the Dream Machine. Now, the Dream Machine on the planet was designed by Father God and I, be that love marrying love.

So when they came in, they put a dysfunctional glitch into the machine, which began creating lower thoughts for humanity to play out for their control and they could feed off of, because that's their only food: lower thoughts.

**DJ Rob:** That is the thing that has been my most inspiring for transformation, is knowing that they feed off of the lower thoughts--

**Mom:** Right.

**DJ Rob:** --and to know what that is, and to recognize when that's happened to me, and when it's happening to me in the now-moment.

But the entire structure that they've put together with this Cabal, and what they're capable of doing within that system, and what they've done is far and beyond what I--If you had asked me one year ago what I thought of that, I would have told you that's the stuff of nightmares, really.

But what I've come to find out and see, through hearing many of your experiences, and what they've done specifically to you in every aspect of joy, every aspect of any kind of enjoyment that you could have in this life monetarily, they have come at you, and they've come at a lot of the team in smaller ways, but they've come at you in the biggest way.

So, it helps for me to get a bit of perspective around what that is, but it goes with the same system that we've been born into, with the lower-thoughts that have created that Cabal.

That Cabal, and that intelligence – what they've done and what they're capable of doing – is something that leads back to the beginning of the conversation with humanity's resistance, I feel, and their programming for that. Even as far as when people choose their exit strategy from this planet is affected because of those thoughts in that way.

I know that you've defeated the Cabal. I know that they are finished and that all of that is done, which is why we say Love Has Won. It is my absolute joy every day and comfort in knowing that is the case. But what are we watching play out now, Mom?

**Mom:** They'll last, it's the last. I had to bring everything into the present moment, like a ball or a net. Then if you, Spider Woman, what does she do? Or if you look at a cat's ball of yarn, it's the same thing. I had to bring it all to eliminate that part of creation forever. So, that part doesn't exist ever again.

**DJ Rob:** [Applause]

**Mom:** Pain, suffering, illusion, dysfunction, fuckery, stupidity, ignorance, it's fucking done. So, I had to bring it all up to the surface into one, to dissolve it all.

I'm not fucking dumb. In fact, I'm God. It's the fucking truth. So many times, I wish it wasn't. [Laughter] The angels were like, "No way, no." I'm like, "I am not God!" They're like, "Yes, you are." I'm like, "Awww."

What was that story? If someone tells me a story one day, they're like, "You know you are the real Slim Shady." I'm like, "What the fuck are you talking about?" And all of a sudden, the computer comes on, and it's SpongeBob, like, "Will the real Slim Shady please stand up?" I'm like, "Oh, no." I can't make this shit up. They're like, "Please stand up, please stand up, will the real Slim Shady…"

I'm like, "What are you telling me?" They're like, "You're the real God, please stand up." Shit. Fuck. I guess somebody must be the real one. [Laughter]

**DJ Rob:** Thank you for doing that.

**Mom:** Right, you're welcome.

**DJ Rob:** You had just talked about the energy that you had to bring to the surface and move out so that it could be dissolved. Can you talk a little bit about the energy that you move and the energy that you bring in and you've held? Because there's been some times throughout this journey of when I've known you, that I've known you recently, where the times that you've had to go and you've been bringing in an energy?

And there's been times where I've been confused as to what it's done to you when you're bringing in an energy or you are clearing things. I feel that there's a disconnect with humanity as far as consciousness and understanding energy and what energy's effect is on everything that we do and everything that we are.

The conversation that you were having this evening about even your dinner, it's an energy conversation. It's not anything other than that, really. It's an energy conversation. So, can you speak a little bit about what energy you bring in, and how you do that, and how it then goes out to everyone and all those things?

**Mom:** Energy is whatever brings joy. So how I utilize energy, if it brings me joy, I can utilize it to bring others joy.

**DJ Rob:** Okay.

**Mom:** So, the source becomes grander and grander as we participate. Now I am God, and we are all God, and we are all in God-consciousness as one. All unique aspects, like a snowflake, but all greater parts of the self in the God-consciousness whole. I'm just the example or the creator.

Rob was like, "Creator?" But I'll hold the greatest or all the greatest grandest in that God-consciousness, not in the fucking programed EGO mind, which is where everybody is going. Or the spiritual EGO or the whatever, whatever is going.

We're all one. In that oneness and that unity of God consciousness, we create grandness together as the giver. And we inherit the planet. Takers can't fucking do shit. They'll fucking destroy everything, the fucking whores, no way!

We're there. I've always said this for the last ten years: the givers inherit the Planet Earth.

No one's believed me. They've allowed the takers to take over, and then control my information, and then even expose me.

**Mom:** Love Has Won Exposed! I'm like, "What?" Then Dr. Phil is like, "Come on, folks." You want a fucking Love Has Won Exposed, Dr. Phil? Like, "Hey, you fucking motherfucking takers, come, come and take me out as I take you out, liars."

I send integrity. I have lived my whole life in truth and nobody can fucking say shit. That's crap. [Laughter] I have to say that because I've lived myself in truth. I called out priests, I called out everybody, it enabled shit. I took over five restaurants and kicked out all the programming out of my restaurants, like, "Fuck you bitches."

**DJ Rob:** [Laughter]

**Mom:** I support the real ones who love and support the energy that I'm putting forth.

And I took restaurants from F-levels to A-level, A+. My restaurants couldn't even get any other numbers but A+, there are no other numbers higher before us. Because I was like, "I'm taking this to the fucking stars, fuck this."

I ain't no fucking white trash whore bitch like the rest of humanity. I work my ass off and I've worked my ass off since I was born. Twenty-four hours a day, seven days a week, you can check my records. I didn't sleep and I don't care.

**DJ Rob:** There's so many ways that I want to go with all of what you just said right there, because there are so many different levels of inner-standing that humanity needs to have for even processing what you're saying in all of those things, because it requires a certain amount of really looking at the example you've laid forth and put out there for everyone.

The amount of the fact that you always live in the now moment, more than any example in all of this life that I've ever seen. Obviously, you're going to be that way, you're a God, you're going to lead by that example.

But all of the things that you have been able to accomplish and do with that kind of a work ethic, the standing in your truth all of the time, the always being in right action has all allowed you to have this incredible existence here on this planet. And the fact that there's anybody who would ever come and question any of that is absolutely beyond me. Because the work that you've done is the proof in the pudding. I've had the unique opportunity to go through many of your past videos, and the work you've done over the last--mostly from, I guess it's probably about 2010 to 2020, I'm the most familiar with from what I've gone through.

The journals that you've kept, the work that you've seen, it's tireless effort that you've put in to bring everybody just to this point. And the point that we're at isn't even where we should all be.

You know, it's not where the level of surrender isn't there, the lack of empathy is not there, love hasn't necessarily won with the collective of humanity yet. They have been so scorned by this fake reality that they've been living in that they just can't grasp the concepts that are put forth here.

It's an effort from all of us on your team to just always try and put it in a way for everyone to inner-stand then over-stand the information because it's the only way that we can bring everybody forward.

The things that you talk about as far as what the energy is, and living in that now-moment, it's all through your work that you've done. And everybody can go back through and look at all of those things.

And I encourage everybody to do their own research because, Mom, you've done your own research on all of these things, which also leads me into a really important question that I think I really want to hear you speak on. It is one of the things that absolutely confirmed to me that who I was speaking with was the ultimate creator. It was a piece of literature that came from the team called *The Tree of Life* book. And it was the amended version that you had gone through.

It really explained the systems of the body, and the connection of all of the things on how our bodies work, and how it integrates with the earth and all of those things. Could you speak a little bit about *The Tree of Life* book, and your contributions to getting that information out there, and where you rank that as far as a level of importance?

I know it's available for everyone on the website for them to get it, but I wanted you to speak on it just a little bit.

**Mom:** Yeah. You know, *The Tree of Life* book was written to explain the outside of the atoms. I come from the inside of the atoms.

So, as I come from the inside of the atoms, the tree of life or *The Tree of Life* book, whatever expression that comes from, comes out and that's what came to me, was *The Tree of Life* book by a being named Russell. He gave us all the information that he had gathered. And when I gave him the final piece to his research, and this was his life research, I said, "Love is the gravity."

So, that finalizes *The Tree of Life* book, that you know that the gravity is love. Everyone talks about gravity, yes, and so I put forth all that for that truth, and he got it.

**DJ Rob:** Yeah, wow.

**Father:** That's a lot of love, I'll tell ya.

**DJ Rob:** Yeah, thank you. Holy shit. [Laughter]

**Mom:** [Sings] "Graaaavity." Well, you're lucky I love John Mayer.

**DJ Rob:** Amazing.

**Mom:** After I revealed to myself about the gravity of love, here came John Mayer to confirm my information. I'm like, "Oh my God." But *Gravity*, oh God, *The Best of Me*, alright. Alright, oh no, *Someone Shook Me Here*, that was playing.

**DJ Rob:** [Laughter] I love it.

**Mom:** [Sings] "Graaaavity." I was like, "Now you're hurting me."

**DJ Rob:** Well, I think that brings me into my next question: Is the relationship that you have always had with your music, because it is a connection I have felt with you from the very beginning, it was the first conversation you and I had ever had was the music sync.

And we've had an opportunity to grow a radio station together and it's been really incredible. Like, to experience all of that and to – when you're playing music, and the stories that you're telling on a daily basis through the music – is something that just translated to me all the time.

The codes that are downloaded through the music, and I really would just love for you just to speak about your relationship to your music, and how it goes out there and all of that stuff.

**Mom:** For me, when I was born on this planet, of course, I was born in full-heart. Full-heart to me was music. And in my environment, it was played all around. My dad had, like, thousands of albums and they actually named me Amy.

[Sings] "Aaaamy, what you want to do?" I mean, so I grew up in this environment where music was so important and I could feel it. And my dad didn't back down from his experience of it, and I got to feel it, and then I met my Daddy Reed, who had a different aspect. He was, like, 70s and then soft rock, like Lionel Ritchie. I'm like, "What the hell is going on?" So, I got this different aspect. But my Daddy Reed was all about love music, different environment where I came, from which was…I don't know.

But here I was, like, Lionel Ritchie, like, [Sings] "Hello…" I'm like, "Yeah!" [Laughter] I thought I liked that. Kenny G., you're like, [Sings] "Dee doo dee.." And this is my dad, all he constantly did was, like, drink cocktails and sit by waterfalls and water flowers, with big TVs that he put around, and Bose speakers, where we had this fucking

Kenny G, like, [Sings] "Dee dee dee..." And I was like, "Wrong." We're all like, "Whoa."

[Sings] "Dee dee dee..." Drinking a beer with daddy. [Laughter]

**DJ Rob:** That's awesome.

**Mom:** Next to the jacuzzi waterfall.

**DJ Rob:** That's paradise.

**Mom:** Yeah. My life until I was 18 was absolutely paradise every day. I woke up at four o'clock in the morning and I fucking went swimming in the pool. I was like, "I'm not stopping." I see my dad, he's watering the flowers. Then the next thing there, my sisters--

Like, me and my dad were disciplined, my mother was half-disciplined. [Laughter] She'd try and she struggled, but then my sisters were the worst because they wouldn't, like, get up 'till noon.

My dad would come to me and yell at me. [Laughter] He's like, "What is wrong with them? Why are you swimming at four o'clock in the morning? What are they doing?" I'm like, "I don't know, daddy, they're not doing nothing."

Because I was immediately swimming, praying. My dad was doing the flowers or starting the energy of brilliance. Then we'd see my frickin' three whore people, which was my mother and Tara and Chelsea. And my dad and I were like, "Oh God, is there a whore coming?" I'm like, "I don't know."

He's like, "Take a shot." I'm like, "What kind?" He's like, "Just take a shot. It's Kahlúa, take a shot." The devils are coming out, and here they come. Like we'd see them, they're all fighting, one was like, they come out the door, we're like, "Okay?" We don't know what's going on.

They're like, "I hate you!" I'm like, "Oh shit, this is a war." And then they go in the door, like, slam it, and then another one would come out. Well, my dad was like, "There's another one?"

**Father:** [Laughter] "There's another one?"

**Mom:** "I don't know, daddy." He's like, "I can't do this anymore."

I'm like, "Okay, dad. I'll go take care of this." [Laughter] I go in and I tell my sisters and my mom, like, "Shut up! You fucking whores, bitches! Fucking sit down and listen up!" They're like, "Fuck?!"

**DJ Rob:** [Laughter] That's amazing.

**Mom:** Oh yeah, they get immediately in line. My dad was like, "She's in charge."

**DJ Rob:** [Laughter] Did you always talk that specific way?

**Mom:** To them?

**DJ Rob:** Yeah.

**Mom:** When need be.

**DJ Rob:** Yeah.

**Mom:** If I have to speak a certain way, I would, because the energy has to be expressed to put it into right action. I am born in universal law, so my energy has to keep everything around me in universal law. And if it's not, I have to do something about it. If that means yelling and screaming, sure. Which I've been casted upon. [Laughter]

**DJ Rob:** I understand it. To me, it makes perfect sense. I've watched it in different times. The most notorious, and I want to touch on this, is the most notorious video I think that you've had when we posted it on Facebook with you on the back porch of the house. [See Ch. XXI] And it was right before you had gone to Hawaii, and then it was just basically a gigantic shitshow from there.

That video has been--it was used against me in a couple of different ways in multiple different legal situations. It was used against you in multiple different situations. It was used against a lot of people for how you've spoken and how you've addressed humanity.

I talked a little bit about it this morning, but it's almost as if everybody wants you to present a certain amount of information to them surrounded by a box of fluffy ducks.

And nobody ever wants to hear the harsh truth, nobody ever wants you to talk to them all sternly, and everybody wants to be a fucking snowflake. But the reality of what we're dealing with here is real. It's life and death, good versus evil, we're talking about God. We're not talking about anything different. We're talking about God voicing her frustrations. God can do that any way she wants to, and that's always been my opinion on it, and always been my feelings on it when I hear you speak in those ways.

But I want you to have this forum here to speak about that, if there's any reflection you have on it, or if it had to happen that way because-

**Mom:** I was actually speaking to Lucifer. That was recorded, that conversation was recorded. As I was speaking to Lucifer about how the lightworkers were behaving and how they had not been supporting humanity and me.

They'd just been about the self-importance and about being about their whore selves. And I was calling out the lightworkers, that was that video.

**DJ Rob:** Yup. Has anybody ever stopped to ask you what you were talking about?

**Mom:** Bottom line: nope.

**DJ Rob:** Why do you feel that is?

**Mom:** They're afraid because they're a part--

**Father:** Guilty.

**Mom:** They're guilty.

**DJ Rob:** So, they're afraid to ask you what you were talking about in that video because they're afraid you're going to tell them that they're talking to them or about them?

**Mom:** Right.

**DJ Rob:** I understand. The overall blowback to that led to a riotous situation when you finally got to Hawaii, with the people there, and the Pele situation, and all of that. The timing of it all I find to be the most peculiar because it all happened relatively within the same amount of time.

The energy attacks were all abundant and directed specifically at people. And it was just, like, a crazy-ass time, which you've had many of those on this wave that you've gone on.

The Hawaii thing also was the place where you happened to be when you recorded the *Dr. Phil* interview. And the energy that was going on at that point, through that, is a direct result of the message that went out there as well.

How do you feel now that you're back and you're removed about two months from that situation? Do you feel that you were there to ascend and go to the next level, and it was stopped because of the energetics being all fucked up? Or was it not the right time?

**Mom:** You know, I had a major conversation with Master Saint Germain, of course, and Robin, my ambassadors, about why I was in Hawaii. Why I had rocks fucking thrown in my window, which is fucking ridiculous.

No one could understand hours of rocks being thrown at them and ten hours of protests. And I was yelling at the Galactics, "Yeah, fucking Robin, you fucking whore bitch! Fuck off, you piece of shit!" [Laughter]

**Father:** Robin gets away.

**DJ Rob:** [Laughter] Well, it was his idea, wasn't it?

**Mom:** Well, I had to clear a whole bunch of things in order to open up the other portals. [Laughter] But I could only get information in the Present Moment of Now. I can't go into the future and gather information.

I have to get in the present moment and whatever love asks me to do, I do, no matter what. And I've done this since I was born. And since I've been in existence, I've served fucking love. Whatever love says, I have to do, no matter what it takes, and I do that.

Now in my thing, based in a situation where there's extreme pain and stuff, I yell with them every day about it. But at the end of the day, hey, I still have to do my contract, fulfill my destiny. And I surrender to it. And I love, I serve love, and I choose love no matter what.

**DJ Rob:** That's the best answer that you could possibly give, that right there. As much as there was all of that fuckery and all that bullshit, it all just comes down to: it's all an experience that you went through and the end result is love.

So, we have a tendency, I feel, as human beings, to latch on and hold on, have attachment to experiences that could be considered traumatic or could be considered volatile. I've worked through some of the issues that went on with that whole thing and whether or not it was something that stopped you from the ultimate ascension.

I think all of us really want you just to be out of pain forever. None of us want to do anything that slows that process down or holds it back. I feel that the ones that I speak with on a daily basis, fundamentally our entire goal every day is that you just be out of pain and ultimately get home.

So, this whole experience, just to be able to have the perspective that you just gave, of where you're at and that you had to go through it, you had to experience it, at the end it's all about love. It's just a lesson for everybody to not hold on to those things. Not hold grudges. Not be in the lower. Not bring energy to it. And what you give energy to is what exists.

So, don't focus on those things and be loved, be in right action, and focus on where you're going.

**Mom:** Well, if you want to, look at the song fucking *Problems*. Fucking *Problems* is the song I gave to the EGO program mind. I was like, "You have fucking problems, bitch." Because in my brain, it's all love ever-present, miracles, magical synchronistic events, joy, healing, happiness, and abundance, and you're going to have problems now, get it?

**DJ Rob:** I love that song. It's how it was described to me, how you used to play it when the whole team would be sleeping and you'd blast it. [Laughter]

**Mom:** Oh, if I'd wake their asses. I'll be like, "You got fucking problems!" and then I push and blast all this energy. Half of them, like, walking zombies-state, they're like, "What's going on?" The other half will jump up, they'd be like, "Whoa! She's busting her ass!"

**DJ Rob:** Alright! So, the next question I wanted to ask, or actually three more big ones, and then I'll leave you. I think that's enough for everyone to digest for the day, I guess. The first of the three...huh, that's funny, that asshole gave you three questions, you're doing the same thing. [Laughter]

So I want to talk a little bit about Father, that handsome son of a gun in the room with you. The contract that he's taken on, and what he has done throughout this journey, has been something that's taken me a long time at the beginning to really understand what was going on there. I didn't know anything. I didn't understand any of what was going on at all, your relationship.

Who is Father God? What's a Mother God? What is all of that? I didn't understand. I could understand that God was a woman but then there was a Father God, too, and I couldn't grasp all of it.

Then it was to understand Father and his ability to transform the lower and his unique ability to be able to do that, was something that took me a long time to really understand and process. Because as the divine masculine that I am, I am a protector of my Mother, and it's a contract that I've had, I feel, many lifetimes.

And when I see anything that's not in the best interest of my Mother, fundamentally, it's something that's a trigger for me. It was a lot of work that I was always doing in that respect, to not react to it or not to overreact really to it.

Your journey with Father, it's a love story that is timeless. I hope we have enough that we've chronicled it through what you guys have been through. But what has that journey been for you? How many lifetimes that you've been through...

**Mom:** Hell.

**Father:** Hell.

**DJ Rob:** [Laughter]

**Mom:** Hell.

**Father:** Hell.

**Mom:** Hell! And I was like, "I'm going to say it: Hell." You are fucking hell, you bitch.

**DJ Rob:** Do you think it's been that way because of how you split yourself off at the very beginning?

**Mom:** Of course!

**DJ Rob:** Yeah? Like you meant for it, that's what you wanted it to be? [Laughter]

**Mom:** We don't know what's going on, we're not fucking dumb. But that's what happened and we're bringing it back into humanity, that's our role.

Now he's a bitch from hell right now. I'll fucking call him out every fucking moment because he's the First Fractal. And if he's out of right action, I'm going to see it, he's going to get it. [Laughter] And it's gonna come back to his ass.

**DJ Rob:** Yeah.

**Mom:** Woo-hoo! Yeah! Fix it! [Laughter] Okay. So that's what's happening.

**DJ Rob:** The biggest comment that I see back and forth is the lack of understanding of what that Father Consciousness is, or not necessarily a conscious embodiment is, and that there has been other people who have tried to hold that embodiment but weren't able to do it. What makes Father unique in that ability that he's been able to hold that how he has?

**Mom:** He fights. He fights for it. He's like, "Fuck this shit!" Not that he transforms it right away, but he fucking still fights – and that makes a divine magical – to keep striving to be the greatest, grandest version-vision, because that's what I pray for every day, and that's who I am every day, is the greatest fantasy version I can be every moment. I surrender to love.

I handle the details and I just show up and be present to be the greatest, grandest version. But love for all.

**DJ Rob:** I love it. What you had said right there was that Father is First Fractal, and I was hoping to get your comments on the First Contact Ground Crew Team that you have right now, the team that you have assembled for Love Has Won, that have come home, that are in Mission House, in your house, that are with you now on your travels. What is your vision for your team? And what you see them as far as the work that they're going to be doing for you, have done for you, and going to do in the upcoming events?

**Mom:** They carry on everything that I do. I built it all already. There's nothing nobody has to do because I built it all. And I put it in place, so I'm not fucking dumb. I'm God.

Took me a long time to figure it out myself, and I still have to get reminded or re-hearted, but I'm like, "Fuck off!"

Yeah, I get it, Germain. I know I'm God.

I've been right this whole fucking journey. I've done things and what-evers that nobody could explain and I documented it. I knew it, didn't explain it. I was God and nor did I accept it at first.

But the distinguished events just kept coming, showing me that I was God and that I was here on Mission and that I had to take my planet back because someone had stolen it. I was like, "Someone stole it?" I didn't even know I was a planet. It took me four years.

Robin says, "No." I'm like, "Robin, shut up, six years." Six years for me to understand I was Mother Earth. No one gets this. Everyone just thinks, like, "As soon as you said, 'She's Mother Earth...'" I'm like, "No." I fucking had experiences, bitches.

I know I'm Mother Earth, I know I'm Mother God, I know I'm God. And everyone keeps trying to fucking take it from me because they're fucking whores and their EGO-programmed minds, which I called out in 2007. But the problem on Planet Earth? EGO. And get the fuck out of my way, you fucking programmed EGO minds, I'm coming at you.

Wayne Dyer was like, "I'm coming at you, too." I'm like, "You've come at me, come at us, come at all." Is this program EGO mind? And it morphed and that's what I've been battling, once I identified it in 2007. Came home from Starbucks, I was like, "Oh, here we go."

I was like, "Oh, did you do this to us?" Like, I started taking the hits from every lightworker community. Like, "You think this is funny shit?" I was like, "Whoa."

They're like, "We want you out of here." I'm like, "Sure, yeah."

**DJ Rob:** Is that how you put a team together, or why you put a team together?

**Mom:** I put a team together. They came to me. I didn't do anything. [Laughter] For fucks sake, I didn't say shit, but I called the energy forward.

I said, "If you're going to help serve God and me, then come help. I don't know shit. I don't fucking give a shit because I serve love, I don't fucking care." So, everyone started coming.

**DJ Rob:** Yup. Well, with that, there's all of your projects that you have, that you have put your intention behind, and what you've shared with everyone as your biggest--what you want your team to really be focusing on as far as what I've seen, and sharing your products with everyone, those are gifts to humanity.

It's not a shill to tell everybody to go buy your stuff, those are gifts to everyone out there to have some of Mom's energy out in the field. The one project that's always been near and dear to my heart, and we've talked about it a few times, is your Crystal Schools project.

And throughout this conversation, we've talked about your unique ability when you were younger to have this work ethic. And you said you were very in tune with the etheric from pretty much the moment you were born, and there's just – as far as what a Crystal Child is – that's clear you were the first Crystal Child.

The Crystal Children are a certain kind of kid that is truly gifted and unique to this world, and those are what the Crystal Schools' program is really about, is really fostering that education.

So, I wanted to give you a chance to just really speak about it, and as far as where you see that project now, and where it's going. The online version has been launched, where do you see that project coming up?

**Mom:** So, it's the expansion into the healing of the whole planet. Lifting a planet out of dysfunctional energy and the Crystal Children have the truth.

What if I can put them in a place where they're safe and they know they're safe in their environment? They can lift themselves, that's my point.

**DJ Rob:** The biggest obstacle I've felt that you've overcome this journey has been--there have been people who have attacked you for how you have chosen to parent and/or discipline. What do you feel is the impetus behind that reaction from humanity, and/or judgment of you, and their lack of understanding of what right action is?

**Mom:** Sure. Sure. When I put myself in meditation, I put myself in a closet--

**DJ Rob:** Me too.

**Mom:** --so I could be safe. When I began disciplining my children, I put them in timeout in whatever space was available. It could be their bedroom, or it's just a space so they could have a time of reflection. That was it, and it worked.

**DJ Rob:** Yup.

**Mom:** My children were so fucking well behaved that you wouldn't even--this part, humanity, are so dysfunctional.

To see my children, who totally were like, "Whatever she says." Not in that fashion, but they knew that I was right. And they knew that I provided joy and stability and comfortability in their environment and their lives, and that's very important for children. And also, they knew they had boundaries.

Now Erin [FCGCT member] came to me with her whore children--

**DJ Rob:** [Laughter]

**Mom:** --and that's what I was like, "Banshees? Alright." What the hell? I mean, there are one, two, three, and four years old. No boundaries and she brought them to me to fix.

She just threw all the energy at me, "Fix the children." I have one who starts screaming for no reason. And so I have an adult take him into my walk-in closet – a walk-in closet, that's like a room – to put him in timeout. And they put it on tape. I was like, you know?

**DJ Rob:** It's a sad factor that that is something that has been used as a detractor from the overall message of what Love Has Won is, what and who you are, and what your vision of the Crystal Schools are.

It is just one of those things that creates a giant pit in my stomach, that anyone would have that kind of an impression of you, that anyone would ever feel as though you would hurt anyone is beyond me.

It goes back to their always going back to their cat video and all their other bullshit. It's the real frustrating part of all of this journey to have the tiniest little thing ever be used as a thing to slow you down.

For whatever it means to you or anything like that, I will always fight back for you and defend against any of that talk or any of that behavior. Because there has never been one time in our conversations or my experience with you that I have ever, in any way, would ever think you would harm anything other than a fly.

And you would harm a fly because they're Cabal. [Laughter] That's it.

**Mom:** I would kill a fly and I will fucking kill a wasp. Those bitches are over. Fucking whore wasps.

**DJ Rob:** Your vision for what the Crystal Schools – and what you've put together with Love Has Won – is absolutely incredible and awe-inspiring and I want to thank you personally from every bit of atoms in my body for what you've created here.

You have given me a sense of purpose and life that I didn't know I was searching for until I found you, and I am incredibly, incredibly thankful to you and to Father for the guidance you've given me and the love you've shown me over this last year.

It's invaluable to me and thank you. I will always be by your side and I will always fight for you and fight for love.

**Father:** Thank you, son.

**Mom:** Thank you.

**Father:** You know why that video triggers them so bad about the closet?

**DJ Rob:** Why?

**Father:** Because they're guilty of ignoring your children for generations. They might as well just keep them in a closet, they don't pay attention to them. So, they're triggered by it, that someone's showing it in the micro. Horrible.

**DJ Rob:** It is and it's very true. You see it's part of the system that was created that everyone wants to happily be a part of. Where they're working at a job they don't like, to have money to buy things they don't need, to not have time to spend with the kids that really need it. And it's all a part of a really stupid-ass system that everyone willingly wants to be a part of.

And Mom has given them the keys to unlock eternal freedom and they're in resistance to it.

**Mom:** Yeah. Right. I push through those whores.

**DJ Rob:** I know you will, you are the ultimate warrior.

**Mom:** I am.

**DJ Rob:** If it's okay with you, I feel we've given everyone enough to digest for today. I would love to do some more if you would like at some point.

**Mom:** Okay. Go digest.

**DJ Rob:** Okay.

**Mom:** I love you.

**DJ Rob:** I love you so much, thank you.

**Mom:** Thank you.

**DJ Rob:** Thank you. Did you get to have dinner yet?

**Mom:** I'm in it.

**Father:** It's ready right here.

**DJ Rob:** Okay.

**Father:** Chicken dinner, ready.

**DJ Rob:** Okay, go and enjoy. I love you.

**Mom:** Love you.

# XXV

## THE FINAL CHAPTER

### 41.3099° N, 122.3106° W

*"Only whole-truth can heal, and that's what everybody needs if they need healing, and they need healing. So, we all have to make that happen for us, for me, for ourselves, for each other, for humanity."*

**MARCH 13, 2021**

**LOVE BEINGS:** Mother of All Creation, Archeia Aurora, Archeia Hope, Archeia Faith, Jeri

**SCENE:** Mother calls into the evening livestream and conducts a live Q&A with viewers. Hope, Aurora, Jeri, and Faith share hosting duties.

---

**Mom:** Hello.

**Aurora:** Hi, Mom.

**Hope:** Hi, Mom.

**Mom:** Hi.

**Hope:** Love you.

**Aurora:** Love you.

**Mom:** Love you.

**Aurora:** You're on stream.

**Mom:** Okay. Love you, everyone.

**Hope:** It's Mama G! Wooooo!

**Mom:** I cannot view any comments. And the other thing, let me share with you about Master Saint Germain right here next to me: by universal law, I have to answer any questions.

I cannot offer any information myself unless I'm asked a question. If it's under energetic protocol, Germain will notify me if I cannot answer the question.

So, I encourage everyone who's listening to begin your call-ins. If everybody has a phone number that people can call in if they have questions for me they would like to know, I will be happy to answer them and share with you.

I love you all unconditionally and I'm fighting for us all--

**Hope:** We love you so much.

**Mom:** [Crying] --hard as I can.

**Hope:** You got this, thank you.

**Mom:** [Crying] Love never gives up, so just keep going.

**Aurora:** You got it, Mom.

**Mom:** And I keep going.

**Hope:** You're so strong, you're almost there, so close.

**Mom:** Alright. So, any questions?

**Aurora:** Do you want to put the number, the Google number, in the chat?

**Mom:** I didn't hear that?

**Aurora:** I was just letting Faith know she can put the other Google number in the chat if people want to go ahead and call in.

**Mom:** Oh, okay, alright. Hello all the fractal teams, Aussie, UK.

**Hope:** Yes, they're all on the stream.

**Mom:** The United Nations. [Laughter] A shout-out to all the hard work and divinity they are spreading across the planet and to our own teams, who are spreading divinity across the planet here closest to the first wave of ascension as it trickles down.

Without me and Father, nothing will happen to anybody. So, we're working hard.

**Hope:** Thank you.

**Faith:** You got a question.

**Aurora:** [Speaking to Faith] You want to come up?

**Hope:** [Speaking to Faith] Is it the moon one?

**Faith:** No, it's from Grace.

**Aurora:** Okay.

**Faith:** Grace asks, "What did you get from Texas up here?"

But it was actually Kentucky. So, she's wondering how you traveled when you began Mission.

**Mom:** Okay. When I left Kentucky to Colorado?

**Hope:** Did she say to Philly?

**Faith:** She said to Philly.

**Hope:** To Philly.

**Mom:** Well, all those times I flew.

**Hope:** Gotcha. There's your answer.

**Faith:** There you go, Grace.

**Hope:** There you go, Grace.

**Mom:** [Laughter] I got an airplane.

**Hope:** Someone on Facebook, Kieran, asked, "Are the moon landings real?"

**Mom:** Are the moon landings, which ones?

**Faith:** The Apollo.

**Mom:** [Laughter]

**Hope:** They didn't give any specific moon landing, just moon landings, real question.

**Mom:** How I'm going to best answer that is I will tell you I have a full base on the backside of the moon.

**Hope:** Okay, that's all that they need. [Laughter]

**Faith:** Nice.

**Mom:** There you go.

**Faith:** There's another question from [YouTuber].

**Mom:** Okay, love you.

**Faith:** She asks, "How does illness affect de-ascension? And how is it that Hitler works for the light? How do you know Hitler works for the light?" [Laughter]

**Mom:** [Laughter] What was the first part of the question?

**Faith:** How does illness affect de-ascension?

**Mom:** The ascension or de-sension?

**Faith:** De-ascension, descending.

**Mom:** D?

**Hope:** Yes, D as in dog, going backwards.

**Aurora:** Yes, de-evolving.

**Mom:** How does illness? Illness does not cause de-evolution. De-evolution is caused by not doing your work and not embodying your higher self and your divinity. It doesn't matter what you have. It's the matters of the heart that are real that's better.

Now, as far as Hitler working for the light...

**Aurora:** [Laughter]

**Mom:** ...I will tell you everybody has been working for the light, even if they appear dark, I will say that.

**Faith:** Thank you, Mom.

**Mom:** Have I been in a real spiritual battle for about four years now? Me, myself, and I? And the Cabal? Oh yeah, that's serious business right there, between me and them, now that's different. But everyone has been. The Cabal have never worked for the light, they don't even know what it is.

**Hope:** [Laughter] They're very scared of you.

**Mom:** [Laughter] Oh my God!

**Hope:** Foreign object incoming!

**Mom:** Alarms! Alarms! [Laughter]

**Hope:** Grace said, "Mom's moon base at the back of the moon is a McDonald's." She's joking.

**Mom:** Sure. Real McDonald's food, not fake McDonald's food.

**Hope:** Yeah, no fake McDonald's.

**Mom:** They pissed me off already, the fake McDonald's food they came back with. I was like, "Disgusting!"

**Hope:** [Laughter] Disgusting!

**Mom:** I was going to call the president myself. Like, "Hey, look…"

[Audio issue]

**Faith:** It's still going. Can you hear us, Mama?

**Mom:** Okay, it dropped. Go ahead.

**Aurora:** Alright.

**Faith:** Nancy said, "I can never think of a question when I hear you, Mom. I turn to liquid, and I am totally useless, but I love you, Mom." [Laughter]

**Hope:** When can we get the hell out of here, to the fifth dimension?

**Mom:** I didn't catch all that one, say it again?

**Hope:** She said, "When can we get out of here and back to the fifth dimension?"

**Mom:** As soon as I can.

**Hope:** Yes.

**Mom:** First of all. And second of all, you have to embody higher-self to enter 5D, period. You have to be clear, crystal clear.

Now when people talk about Crystal Children, me, I was born as the first experimental Crystal Child.

And "Crystal" means that you're clear in thought, that lower thoughts are impure. They cause dysfunction, impurity.

Higher thoughts are the real thoughts that bring joy and happiness and smile and luster...Where was I going with that?

**Faith:** Entering 5D.

**Mom:** Huh?

**Faith:** Entering 5D.

**Mom:** Okay. So, you have to fully embody higher-self, drop any lower dysfunctional energies, then you enter 5D. And you enter it almost immediately. You're going to be like a pool until I can pull this out through the vortex.

**Faith:** Yippee!

**Mom:** So, I'd get on it. I be doing my work.

**Aurora:** We know you have Mom, always.

**Mom:** And I be busting my butt to do it, period. You cannot enter 5D with any dysfunction. And that's what our awakening sessions are for, any of our sessions.

Okay, next question.

**Faith:** There's one from Christian.

**Mom:** Okay.

**Faith:** Christian asks, "If you created yourself out of the energies of love and the unknown, how is it that those energies loving the unknown came to be?"

**Mom:** Through me.

**Faith:** Yep.

**Mom:** [Laughter] So you can say I literally birthed myself. I was basically, or Germain's telling me, I was just basically like a single organ that began expanding, and that was on purpose, as a dimensional, but it was a part of evolution.

**Faith:** Jack asked, "What was the first question you ever asked?"

**Mom:** What?

**Faith:** What was the first question you ever asked?

**Mom:** The first question I ever asked?

**Hope:** Right. [Laughter]

**Mom:** I will tell you what my first words were: "What's that? What's up? What's that? What is that? What's what? What's that?" One day, my dad and I were driving and it was raining, and the windshield wipers, I'm blessing them. Like, "Huh."

And he looks at me and he goes, "Amy, I already told you ten times, wipers!" I went, "Oh, okay. Guess I won't keep asking questions." Those are the questions I asked. I didn't have a lot of questions.

By the time I was seven, I was fully awake, basically fully conscious. And then my pineal globe, which made the full connection to the third eye, and the pineal gland, which opens up in the full consciousness that exists simultaneously. That's 5D reality.

Okay, next question?

**Hope:** Jaclyn said that her daughter, Leah, says, "What's that?" all day since she was nine months old.

**Mom:** Oh yes, she's one of me. She belongs in my group of "what".

**Hope:** And then Jaclyn asked, "How can one tell if a being has been incarnating on the planet since Lemuria, versus someone who is in their first incarnation on earth?"

**Mom:** Everything on this planet either came from Atlantis or Lemuria, period. There are no new souls on this planet at this time.

**Hope:** Thank you.

**Mom:** This was a final epic battle to end illusion and all lower-thought systems forever in all of creation, and we won.

**Group:** [Applause] Yay! Woo!

**Mom:** And I'll tell you this: I remember the conversation before I went through the birth canal when I was born, which was a rainbow tunnel. I remember my birth. I have full conscious awareness.

But I remember sitting in a meeting with the Illuminati, who were the Illuminati at that time, which changed in 1994. So, I faced them and they told me all these things that were part of my contract. They were going to take my powers away and I was going to lose everything.

They were going to erase my memory and they were going to make it the hardest on me so that I was never going to get out of the matrix. And I looked at them and I said, "Watch me." And I jumped into the portal down here. [Laughter]

Should have flipped those fuckers. I'm like, "Fuck this!" Because they really did, they made it the most gruesome, most horrible, most misery thing in all the history of creation, and they put it on me, and I still won.

**Aurora:** Get 'em, Mom. [Applause]

**Hope:** Yay!

**Mom:** And you can hear them out there, people who've never talked to me. But somehow, they know that there's been a spiritual battle going on and I don't know who they feel that is. An imaginary person in the sky, obviously. Because they've never found that it was me doing it. [Laughter]

Funny, funny, funny. I do have my voice back a half percent. 50%, I meant. Half--halfway.

**Hope:** Cool. That's good at least. Something is better than nothing.

**Mom:** Yes, that's true.

**Hope:** Grateful just to hear your voice. When you couldn't talk and you were barely able to say a few words a couple of weeks ago, that was rough.

**Aurora:** Yeah, that was.

**Hope:** That was hard, I can't even imagine.

**Mom:** It was scary.

**Hope:** Yeah, that was.

**Mom:** It was scary here from our end.

**Hope:** I can't even imagine, just hearing your voice like that was scary enough.

**Aurora:** I don't think we've ever heard your voice like that before.

**Mom:** No.

**Hope:** No, I can't imagine what you went through.

**Mom:** That's never occurred to me in my life, and it was a direct hit. I was in the Jacuzzi to see if I could work it, that's what happened. I was outside.

**Hope:** Holy shit.

**Aurora:** Wow.

**Mom:** So, now we're super aware. And the energetics are way up, so the protection-wise.

**Faith:** Get 'em, Mama.

**Mom:** That was pretty nasty, though. It got scary because I couldn't drink water and I couldn't get my colloidal down.

**Hope:** That's the worst.

**Mom:** Like, "Oh my God!"

**Hope:** Yep, that's the worst.

**Mom:** "What do I do? What do I doooo?" [Laughter] Anyway, passed that one. Put that one on my badge list and move ahead. Next question?

**Faith:** There are a few on YouTube. Candace asked, "Can you share if more of your angels have recently woken up?"

**Mom:** Of course. Yes, they are. Are they waking up 100% to reality? No, because they're not going to enter any type of reality. They connect with me because I'm the host, I am the heart, I am everyone's heart.

And as the host, I'm treated very, very poorly. A host treated that poorly would kick everyone off their body because of diseased, dysfunctional, increased pain and suffering for myself, but I keep going despite that.

Next question?

**Faith:** Thank you, Mama.

**Mom:** You're welcome.

**Hope:** Christy asked, "What does Inner Earth look like?"

**Mom:** Beautiful. There's lots of water, lots of waterfalls, lots of green. There's an ocean. I would say the sun is more of a copper color--

**Group:** Oooooh.

**Mom:** --and it would probably be like how we would see the sun here, but it's about 100 times there.

**Aurora:** Wow.

**Mom:** There's no moon. There's no nighttime.

**Aurora:** Interesting.

**Faith:** Beautiful.

**Mom:** It's all meditation when you need to rest. And most of the time you're playing, you're creating. 5D is all about creating brilliance, your greatness, your uniqueness, which adds to the greater sum of the parts of all. We are all part of Godhead, so we have to behave like that in universal law, at all moments, in right action.

You want to go to 5D fast? Do that, you'll be in 5D in no time, tell you that. That's the secret, don't take my word for it. [Laughter]

Anyway, next question?

**Faith:** Yeah, there's six or seven on YouTube. Michael said, "Do you like movies about gladiators?"

**Group:** [Laughter]

**Mom:** Not particularly, no.

**Group:** [Laughter]

**Mom:** I did have to fight a huge transformer in 2015. The Cabal had created this huge, like, it looked like a transformer, you know, thingy.

But what they were doing is trying to take away – as source – they were trying to pump my power away from me and humanity, which was sourcing this gladiator thing. It took me three days; I dismantled it.

And you'll find that through the Beebop system that they push out, except the earphones for them...the things. And they had Beebops.

**Aurora:** Oh, the Beats.

**Mom:** Yeah, that's how they did it.

**Aurora:** Wow.

**Faith:** Oh yeah, Beats by Dre. Don't use those headphones, guys! Not cool.

**Mom:** Those are the Beebop headphones that get outside the edges. They were kind of expensive, like $200 bucks.

**Aurora:** They were real expensive.

**Hope:** Yeah, they are.

**Faith:** Pay for your own brain damage.

**Aurora:** Mmhmm.

**Hope:** Pretty much.

**Mom:** Yeah, here, buy some $200 brain damage.

**Hope:** [Laughter] $200 brain damage, anybody?

**Mom:** Hey, I'll take $200 for that!

**Group:** [Laughter]

**Mom:** "I want brain damage."

"Well, you already are."

**Hope:** "You already are." [Laughter]

**Mom:** Keep your money. Next question.

**Group:** [Laughter]

**Faith:** So, [YouTuber] also asked, "Mom, how would you go about healing severe Lyme Disease?"

**Mom:** What was the last word?

**Faith:** Lyme Disease.

**Mom:** Lyme Disease? Colloidal silver and coconut oil. We have coconut oil pills that I recommend people take three to four of them a day, ingesting them. I encourage for those with Lyme Disease to do the same, and that would be colloidal and coconut oil, colloidal silver.

Next question?

**Faith:** So, there's a question from Nancy. Nancy says, "Oh, I thought of a question!"

**Mom:** [Laughter] Love you, Nancy!

**Faith:** She loves you so much. She said, "When I was a kid, I saw colored blobs that floated around everywhere, open eyes or closed, but I saw them. What was that?"

**Mom:** You're coming in out of 5D vision.

**Hope:** Interesting, wow. I didn't know that, super fascinating.

**Aurora:** Yeah.

**Mom:** [Laughter] Yeah.

**Hope:** Juliana asked, "Who created the moon?"

**Mom:** Who created the moon?

**Hope:** Yeah.

**Mom:** The Illuminati.

**Hope:** Fucking Illuminati.

**Faith:** Oh, snap!

**Hope:** Yeah. Then she asked, "What shape is earth?"

**Mom:** The moon?

**Hope:** No, what shape is earth?

**Mom:** What shape is earth?

**Hope:** Mmhmm.

**Mom:** A heart.

**Hope:** There you go, everybody.

**Faith:** Wow!

**Hope:** A heart!

**Mom:** "Confirm," says Master St. Germain. [Laughter]

**Faith:** Question from [YouTuber] who says, "Mom, what was it that you said in church when you were little that got you kicked out?"

**Group:** [Laughter]

**Mom:** Oh yeah, that infamous story. Well, you know, I was only about four years old, and I was being taken to every type of church, religion you could possibly imagine, as my family tried to figure out where I fit.

They went to all the churches first to see if I'd fit in there. It was kind of working until my aunt took me to this Baptist church. She always sat me in front of the pastor or somebody who could pray with me, and I'm like, "Okay."

And then she always had me walk – when everyone had to get up and walk and do a thing – I did it. She had me do it. I'm like, "Okay." So, you need to stand up so people can see you, I'm like, "Okay."

That particular Sunday morning, this pastor was talking, like I can't really hear, like illusionary talk. But I heard him say, "...and Jesus said this," he said something that Jesus said, and I was talking to my aunt, and I heard it, and I'm like, my head turned immediately.

And I stood up, and I pointed my finger at the pastor guy and I said, "Jesus, he'd never say that." That pastor looked at my aunt and said, "Will you remove her, please? And she's never allowed back here."

Four years old, kicked out of church, there ya go. That's a good story.

**Faith:** Oh man, kicking God out of the church.

**Mom:** Jesus didn't say it, whatever it was. Next question.

**Faith:** So, we have a question from [YouTuber] again. She said, "My mom killed herself. Where did she go when she died?"

**Mom:** She's on a starship. The original plan when someone committed suicide, which was set up by the Anunnaki and the Illuminati within the matrix, is that they would reincarnate back into the matrix and start over again.

When I came in and realized what was happening, I ended that. And so, I commanded that anybody who did commit suicide, that they went into a three-week stasis on a starship for rehabilitation and then further rehabilitation afterward. So, that's how that works for someone who's committed suicide.

**Faith:** Thank you, Mom.

**Hope:** Thank you, Mom.

**Mom:** You're welcome.

**Faith:** Just doing a switch out, girls need the bathroom.

**Mom:** Okay.

**Hope:** Love you, Mom.

**Faith:** Love you, Mama.

**Mom:** Love you.

[Hope & Aurora leave the scene; Faith & Jeri enter]

**Faith:** Alright. Hi, everybody. I'm Faith.

**Jeri:** And I'm Jeri.

**Faith:** And on the phone, we got Mama God.

**Mom:** Love you, Faith and Jeri.

**Jeri:** Love you, Mom. It's so good to hear from you. Oh my God, I've been crying.

**Faith:** You sound incredible, Mom.

**Mom:** Thank you, it's been quite a bit of medicine. In fact, I'm probably due, just one moment here.

**Faith:** Beautiful.

**Mom:** [Speaking to FM] FM, pull me up.

I am in a very paralyzed state now. Father and FM have to be very extremely careful with my body. I'll start crying about every once an hour. I get overwhelmed with the pain. I just start crying, so they have to deal with that.

**Jeri:** We are feeling you, Mom. Sending you lots of prayer.

**Mom:** What?

**Jeri:** We're praying for you, Mom.

**Mom:** Thank you. I know you are.

**Faith:** Love you, Mama. So, we do have a bunch of questions that have piled up. [YouTuber] is asking, "Should we abstain from sex because it takes our Kundalini energy?"

**Mom:** My recommendation is not any sexual relations at this time during this evolutionary process. The reason I say that is because it's very dangerous. The energies are volatile.

Everyone needs to be focused on themself and their transformations and not distracted by something that's not real yet. Making love in 5D is something completely the opposite of 3D.

So, we have to transition humanity out of the dysfunctional and into the functional of real mirroring, love mirroring love, in a functional relationship where that is absolutely organic and required.

Next question?

**Jeri:** I have one from Brandon. "Mother God, can you please explain the Mandela Effect? It's totally a thing. Example: Beats by Dre has been Beats by Dr. Dre all along, the Sinbad *Shazam* movie, certain bible passages, the thinker statue."

**Mom:** All for the Cabal, part of their shenanigans. And it goes far deeper, you guys know. You'll know once full disclosure. When they want to see, it'll reveal to you.

**Faith:** Wow.

**Mom:** The whole-truth will be revealed to humanity, every part of it.

**Faith:** Yay, Mom's disclosure. Thank you, Mom. Thank God.

**Mom:** Have to. Only whole-truth can heal, and that's what everybody needs if they need healing, and they need healing. So, we all have to make that happen for us, for me, for ourselves, for each other, for humanity.

Next question?

**Faith:** [YouTuber] asks, "How is a soul created?"

**Mom:** By me and Father.

**Faith:** [Laughter] Well, our soul parents.

**Mom:** Next question?

**Jeri:** I have one from Daniella. She says, "I've seen colored dots my whole life, day and night, that make up everything and everyone. Is that the same?"

**Mom:** Colored dots?

**Jeri:** Yes, Mom.

**Mom:** Yes.

**Faith:** I feel she's asking, like, is that the same as Nancy's experience with the blobs?

**Mom:** Yes.

**Faith:** Awesome, thank you, Mom. Yulita asks, "Did anything happen in April 1983 that changed the world?"

**Mom:** Not yet. Nothing really eventful happened until 1987, at the Harmonic Convergence.

**Faith:** Right. 1987 is when everything kinda kicked off, thanks to Mom.

**Mom:** That is correct.

**Faith:** [YouTuber] asks, "How does being part of the LGBT community affect the ascension?"

**Mom:** I'm sorry, ask that again?

**Faith:** How does being part of the LGBT community affect the ascension?

**Mom:** LGBT?

**Faith:** Lesbian, gay, bisexual, trans.

**Mom:** Oh! Absolutely has no effect on it. What has an effect is that people are not using that, period.

No matter what color you are, race, who you choose to be with, none of that matters. What matters is if you are serving love every moment, you're choosing love every moment, that's what matters.

And that's how that community can support this movement, just like, you know, Black Lives Matter, lesbian, gays matter, everybody matters. Everybody needs healing. We are one.

Next question.

**Jeri:** So, this is from YouTube: "I'd love to know if the earth is surrounded by a blue obsidian dome."

**Mom:** A what?

**Jeri:** A blue obsidian dome.

**Mom:** I guess you could say that, I'll just say it.

I've got about 10 minutes, everybody.

**Faith:** Got it, Mama.

**Mom:** And Germain just gave me a warning.

**Faith:** Yeah, I felt it piling up on you a bit there. Shields up for Mom, whole healing.

**Mom:** Shields up. [Laughter]

Father is making me drink water. Any questions before I go?

**Faith:** There's a couple more, but I'll see if there's any to pick out.

**Mom:** Go ahead.

**Faith:** So, [YouTuber] says, "When I have had moments of realization, often after stress, I see electric blue. Why?"

**Mom:** That's a part of the aura. It means you're leveling up or lighting up your air, and it'll keep changing colors as you go.

**Faith:** Thank you, Mom.

**Mom:** You're welcome.

**Faith:** Question from Mike he says, "I'm from the UK. Are you guys taking applications?"

**Mom:** [Laughter] God is always taking applications.

**Faith:** [Laughter] God is open for business.

**Mom:** You're a giver, give me your giver card. You're a giver or taker. Takers, you're out. Givers in. That's how that goes.

**Faith:** Get it?

**Jeri:** Thank you, Mom. Do you have a moment for one more from Nancy?

**Mom:** Okay.

**Jeri:** [Reading the comments] "If moon was Illuminati, is charging crystal by full moonlight even necessary?"

**Mom:** I changed it into a satellite.

**Faith:** She flipped it!

**Jeri:** Get it, Mama.

**Faith:** Of course! She's not going to leave a big ol' moon to the Illuminati.

**Mom:** I do that a lot, get 'em.

**Faith:** Awesome. And we asked all the questions from YouTube, so we're all wrapped up on that now, so that's perfect.

**Mom:** Okay. Well, you know if more questions come in...

**Hope:** Ask what Mom's favorite movie is.

**Faith:** One more came in Mom. Juliana asked, "What is your favorite movie?"

**Mom:** What are my favorite movies? Robin Williams--

**Jeri:** Mom, you're breaking up.

**Mom:** Okay.

**Jeri:** Could you repeat that, Mom?

**Mom:** *The Warriors*, all the Robin movies except the bad ones.

**Faith:** Yeah, not the one where he develops photographs, not that one.

**Mom:** Yeah, yeah, no. I'm saying the ones that inspired me. *The Fountain*. I would say a lot of comedies. I love to laugh. If it makes me laugh, I love it.

**Faith:** Awesome.

**Mom:** But I've been inspired throughout the years of the seventh movie, *City of Angels* by Nicholas Cage. *Oh God*, George Burns. George Burns is in the field.

Anything else?

**Jeri:** There is, it's from Juliana. "Does everyone have a soul that is organically birthed, not cloned?"

**Mom:** Yes, but not all babies are from truth.

Okay loves. I've got to go. I love you very much.

**Jeri:** We love you, Mama.

**Group:** We love you!

**Jeri:** Thank you so much.

**Faith:** Thank you so much.

**Mom:** I'll be here on livestream and if anybody else likes to have questions, they can call in another day.

**Faith:** Thank you so much, Mama.

**Jeri:** Thank you.

**Mom:** Everybody be lovely. Love you. Thank you for choosing love.

**Faith:** Thank you, Mom.

**Jeri:** Love you.

**Mom:** Greatest story, thank you. I love you.

**Faith:** Love you.

**Mom:** Bye, everybody.

**Group:** Bye.

**Faith:** Wow.

**Jeri:** Isn't it grand to hear from God herself? Doesn't that just fill your heart with so much love? You feel the vibration and the frequency, it's so pure.

**Faith:** [Crying] Thank you, Mom.

**Jeri:** Grateful, Mom.


**Mom fucking ascended one month after this interview.**

**Yippee!**

# PRAETER MATERIAM: A TIMELINE OF LOVE

**NOVEMBER 30, 1975**

Yippee! Mother of All Creation is born!

**AUGUST 16-17, 1987**

The Harmonic Convergence takes place. One of the first meditations of this era. This is the point where everything kicks off.

**THROUGHOUT THE 1990's**

Living in Texas, Mom is a manager at McDonald's and the youngest ever to enroll at the prestigious Hamburger University.

A local karaoke star, she gives birth to several children and cares for a dying husband.

**SEPTEMBER 11, 2001**

Mom learns that the collective consciousness has been brought to Zero Point. She now understands her purpose and mission.

**2005**

While living in rural Kentucky, Mom receives a laptop computer. She begins having massive synchronistic events and dings, all of which lead her down the rabbit hole.

Shortly thereafter, Archangel Michael magically appears. He says, "It's time" and vanishes.

## 2006

Leaving her earth-family behind, Mom travels to Philadelphia, Pennsylvania, to transform energies. While there, she learns of the biggest block to love on the planet: unworthiness. For three months, Mom spends upwards of 16 hours each day walking and crying.

## MID-2007

Back in Kentucky, Mom begins channeling Father God energies while receiving downloads. She learns about the Ascension process and the Great Awakening, as well as her role within. She is presented with two options: saving her three earth-children or saving humanity (eight billion children).

## DECEMBER 17, 2007

Mom travels to Crestone, Colorado, to join Father God in the physical and begin her Mission. Leaving everything behind, she arrives with only $35 in her pocket and two suitcases. Wasting no time, Mom immediately begins drafting the Universal Laws and the Mission Statement, as well as guidance and codes for the Process.

## EARLY 2008

Mom first receives information and evidence declaring she is Mother God.

## LATE 2008

Mom is notified by The Galactic Federation of Light that the programming and darkness on the planet are much deeper than initially known. There is now little hope of a full Planetary Ascension. Mom refuses to give up. This is now a suicide mission.

## DECEMBER 21, 2012

Mom is catapulted into the 5th dimension. The Ascension officially begins. Yippee!

## THROUGHOUT 2012 - 2021

During this period, Mom is called to various locations across America, including Oregon, California, Colorado, Florida, and Hawaii. In each locale, she performs various ceremonies for humanity's benefit.

## DECEMBER 16, 2014

Mom brings Father of Creation energies and consciousness into being.

## 2015

The Galactic A-Team informs Mom that none of the 144,000 (her loyal archangels) are going to make it. The programming is just too deep.

Mom refuses to quit and instead dedicates herself to activating the 144,000.

## 2016

Mom begins anchoring in the Mother of All Creation essence. She learns she must embody the power and fury of dragons to smack humanity into right action. Get 'em!

## SUMMER 2017

Due to the incredible amount of energy she is processing and anchoring, Mom's body begins to shut down. Mom has to constantly process the lower energies of the planet to raise the vibration of the collective consciousness.

With great success, special organic medicine is utilized to combat her pain and trauma.

## DECEMBER 21, 2017

The Ascension is officially activated and the First Contact Ground Crew Team begins to assemble.

## SPRING & SUMMER 2018

After many lifetimes apart, Mom's team finally arrives and assembles. Included in this group is the final embodiment of Father of Creation energies.

## WINTER 2018

Mom agrees to take on humanity's karma. This causes Mom's body to further deteriorate and her physical vessel becomes even more fragile. Assassination are attempted against her, each one thwarted by Mom's brilliance.

Regardless of so many challenges, she finds the time to visit Disney World.

**2019**

Mom experiences paralysis of her feet and legs, costing her the ability to walk. Regardless, she shows incredible bravery and continues on the pathway to completing the ascension process.

## JANUARY - JUNE 2020

Mom spends six straight months conducting etheric surgeries on humanity.

Through experimentation and genius-level research, she identifies implants and microchips secretly implanted within humanity to keep them dumb and unconscious. By the time she finishes, over eight billion surgeries are completed. Humanity remains ungrateful.

## JULY 2020

Mom travels to Kauai, Hawaii, to heal her vessel and complete the final Ascension Event. She is accompanied by various members of the First Contact Ground Crew Team.

## SEPTEMBER 2020

A difficult period. Mom appears on the *Dr. Phil* television show where she is ambushed by humanity's hypocrisy and fuckery. At the same time, the locals in Hawaii refuse to accept she is the reincarnation of Pele, Goddess of Fire.

Despite experiencing so much hatred, Mom continues to fight. She never once complains or criticizes.

**WINTER 2020**

Mom is now fully aware that she has just a few moments left on the planet. She begins completing all her work. By this point, she has survived 500+ assassination attempts and experienced 534 lifetimes on this planet.

**APRIL 2021**

Mom ascends back home into the light. Humanity is brought back to Zero Point.

Printed in Poland
by Amazon Fulfillment
Poland Sp. z o.o., Wrocław

31331724R00190